BACKPACKING BLUES

Adventures of a
Brown Backpacker

SOUMYA MUKHERJEE

INDIA • SINGAPORE • MALAYSIA

ISBN 979-8-89498-834-4

CONTENTS

Dedication

My long suffering co travellers, initially Teji, my partner,
and later my two kids, who shared my passion, and
now are solo backpackers to extraordinary places around
the globe

Dedicated to the readers of my travel blogs who insisted
that I try to make a book out of the rambling tales, and
my long suffering co travellers in these adventures, my
wife and my two daughters

ACKNOWLEDGEMENTS

Cover Illustrator: Parmita Mukherjee

Parmita is a graduate of the Shrishti school of art and design

Editor: Malvika Singh

Malvika is a lawyer by training and literateaure by passion

Chapter 1
FIRSTS

There are many firsts in our lives that leave an indelible mark on our psyche, staying fresh in our memory for a lifetime. We remember these experiences, the sight, the sounds, the emotions associated with it, even the smells linger in our memory. I am trying to recount these firsts in my life, but not chronologically.

The first view of the sea

I must have been about four or five. The place was Puri in Orissa. We had come by train, and took a rickshaw going towards the beach where we had rented a house. I had heard so much about the sea and seen pictures, and I could feel the salt on my lips, smell the peculiar salty air, and hear the constant undulating roar of the surf, before we crested a rise, and there it was, in all its majestic glory, the vast expanse of blue, with the breakers racing towards the beach, topped by white surf, and the yellow sand beach disappearing in the surf.

Nothing had prepared me for the grandeur. Since then I have been to numerous beaches all over India and in four different continents, had a sea journey, and learnt scuba diving; even been rescued after a boat capsize in the sea, but this first vision from early childhood remains vivid in my mind.

The first view of snow peaks

I was six or seven. We had taken the train to NJP in North Bengal. From there we hired a jeep to take us up to the hills. As we drove out of the city, we could see the layers of green hills and further grey ranges behind them disappearing into the clouds. Suddenly the clouds lifted, and there, shining in the sunlight, the mighty Himalayas displaying her crown of snow peaks, the Kanchanjungha Range.

All these years later, having seen all the major snow peaks in the Himalayas, the Alps and even mount Kilimanjaro in Africa, the memory of that first sight, with the cool crisp air and the smell of pines, remains fresh in my mind.

The First flight

I was in class six. We were off to our annual vacation to Darjeeling. The airplane was a propeller driven Fokker Friendship. I was excited beyond imagination. The roaring noise, the feeling of your stomach being left behind while the body is moving on, the ground rushing past and suddenly growing smaller, the bird's eye view, the white clouds enveloping us, the ears getting blocked, toffees served, the entire thrilling journey is vivid in my memory, and all the frequent flyer points and intercontinental travel will not fade the memory of this first flight.

The First sight of....

Snow... Mountains of it, heaped on either side of the road on the way to Rohtang pass, the road, a tunnel between walls of snow. We went tobogganing, made snowmen, had snow ball fights and even unsuccessfully tried to learn skiing. Left feeling sore, cold, wet and excited. Numerous treks in the snow later, which included being trapped by an avalanche in Drass, this remains vivid in my mind.

Snowfall... On the trek to Kedarnath. The first exciting flakes, cold and crisp to touch, melt with a tingle on the tip of the tongue that soon turned into a thick flurry that deteriorated into a life threatening blizzard. But that's another story. And one that will stay with me till death.

The Taj Mahal...

Even after hearing and reading so much and all the pictures, the first view through the arch of the gateway is special. It gives you goose bumps. It was on a tour with my cousins while doing the very touristy golden triangle and numerous visits later, still remains fresh in my memory

The Niagara Falls...

Here too all the pictures and descriptions don't prepare you for the majestic sight the feel of cold spray and the roar of the gigantic Horseshoe Falls on the Canadian side. Like the sea you can hear it before you see it. And the Maid of the Mist takes you up close and personal. There's a walk behind the falls as well, a unique experience, and a scary zip line that swings you close to the wall of roaring water. I tried out everything.

The Undersea World...

No amount of national geographic channel binge viewing can prepare you for the real thing. Once you have gotten over the fear of choking or drowning and have learnt to manoeuvre yourself with the flippers, scuba diving is a dream come true. Weird and colourful sea creatures floating by up close and ignoring you. You feel like an invisible alien in a completely different world. This happened at Jolly Buoy in the Andaman's before the tsunami ruined the reefs. I have tried scuba diving later too but nothing beats the first experience

The Everest from up close

My daughter gave me this privilege when I was visiting her in Kathmandu Nepal. A tiny ramshackle 16 seater aircraft of a local airline took us on the pre-dawn flight over the mighty Himalayan ranges at low altitude. It was incredibly exciting. Finally when we circled the Everest it was just another peak like many but it was an emotional experience. People started weeping. Champagne was served. We could all visit the cockpit by turns to get the full unrestricted view of the top of the world from up close and personal. Will never ever forget experience

The Tiger in the wild

Having read stories of the Indian jungle since childhood and being an avid watcher of geography channels I longed to see for myself the king of the jungle the royal Bengal tiger in her own domain. But every visit to the tiger sanctuaries proved futile. Till at last on my eighth visit at Bandhavgarh she finally gave darshan. And what an awesome experience. Six feet away from elephant back we witnessed a battle between two young princes over a kill.

After that I have sighted the big cat almost a dozen times but that first view with the putrid smell of the carcass the roar in my ears is as fresh as if it happened yesterday.

The Great animal migration of Serengeti..

In my childhood I had seen a film called Serengeti shall not die. Ever since visiting this place in person remained on my bucket list. I followed the event on geographic channels, saw all the films, and there are plenty, both documentaries and feature films, read all the books I could get starting with a childhood classic Chander Pahar or mountain of the moon. So finally we blew up our savings and went on a family vacation to Tanzania.

The first view of the graceful giraffes loping ahead and thousands of zebras gnus and antelope blocking the way all the way to the horizon, the crocodiles waiting in the river, the lions on the kill, it was an orgy of Kodak moments jostling for space in our memory. This has spoiled all future trips to wildlife sanctuaries as everything will be an anticlimax after this

Then there is the experience of para gliding off the mountains and white water rafting in the Rapids. Both experiences of being in elements alien to you and the adrenaline rush of flirting with death are heady and never pale, but the first experience is something that you never forget, much like the first experience of making love.

I have written about many of these experiences earlier and will write about the others too in separate stories.

This is a story about the first experiences that never fade.

Chapter 2
RAIN

When we became parents of two young children our backpacking days became rarer but the travel lust remained.

Now we owned a car and often took road trips to the nearby states covering Himachal and Uttarakhand in summer and Rajasthan and Madhya Pradesh in winter.

This time we were in Chail. Approachable by a narrow road and in the middle of pristine forests with only the converted palace of the colourful Maharaja as the only hotel this was an ideal getaway in Himachal.

We took long walks in the woods and lazed around. The weather was sunny and pleasant. One day we decided to take a day long trek to a nearby hilltop where shepherds had a shrine.

It was a long climb but we took it easy and the view from the top made the effort worthwhile.

We relaxed on the meadow on top and had the packed lunch we were carrying. Gradually we noticed that it seemed to be getting darker. There were thick black clouds rolling across the sky. Rain seemed imminent. We had an option of taking shelter in the deserted shrine but not knowing how long we would be stuck and not relishing the idea of going back down the trail in the dark we decided to hurry back. As it was mostly downhill and a fair-weather road existed we assumed that we will make it back safely.

So picking up the younger kid piggyback we set off at a brisk trot, the elder child gleefully leading the way.

But before long the cloud burst caught us with a ferocious violence.

With lightning flashes and thunder in the background taking shelter under the trees didn't seem advisable. Anyway we were reluctant to leave the track and enter the dark woods. The track was fast turning into slush making running impossible. We made our way as fast as possible occasionally slipping and soaked up to the skin.

Initially my daughters were enjoying the rain but now it was becoming scary and extremely uncomfortable. We were shivering with cold and fatigue and slipping in the slush.

After what seemed like ages, we felt the metalled road under our feet and felt relief. The going got easier and we knew that the village wasn't far.

When finally a few huts loomed up in the mist, we felt elated. There was the possibility of shelter. We ran the rest of the way and huddled under the porch of the first hut.

Then the flap covering a hut a small distance away opened up, and a few people came towards us. They were carrying plastic sheets and umbrellas and took us, well covered, into that hut, which was a tea shop.

There we sat next to a blazing fire and dried ourselves on some cloth the kind hosts provided, while the rain thundered outside. We were also provided rough blankets to cover ourselves up.

We were also offered some dry clothes of the tea shop owner's family and could change behind some sheets strung up. The kids were bundled into those poncho like garments hill people wear. The clothes may not have been very clean, for in the hills washing is an infrequent activity, but getting out of the soaked clothes was a lifesaver.

Hot tea was served and hot milk for the kids. My tea was also laced with some army rum.

Dressed in dry warm clothes, with hot tea, mathi (a form of desi biscuits) and pakoras inside us, sitting by a crackling fire, while the rain roared outside; this was heaven. The hopeless struggle in the rain, cold and wet, of a few minutes ago seemed to be a bad dream.

In the meanwhile, a boy had been sent swathed in plastic sheets to the hotel to summon a car, and in a while the hotel van was there to pick us up.

With profuse thanks we left, looking like people in fancy dress. The hosts refused any money, but when we sent back the clothes we sent chocolates for the children.

Many years later, I was visiting that area for a conference. Many resorts had come up, and there was a metalled road to the shrine, while the shack had been replaced by a garish temple, and a mainstream goddess reigned instead of the spirit goddess of the shepherds. The tea shop had closed, the owner no more, and the boy was now a waiter at one of the resorts. Progress I suppose cannot be held back, but I missed the idyll of old.

All I had now was the memories of that rainy visit to these hills.

Chapter 3

SNOW

Being born in a hot semi tropical country in the humid plains of Bengal, I was always fascinated by the idea of snow. Seeing pictures of snowfall, snowmen and snowball fights in books, making snowmen out of cotton wool in the crafts class, singing Christmas carols dealing with snow in our Catholic School and seeing snow covered fields in films served to heighten this longing. In my imagination, the cool soft feeling of snow seemed to be bliss especially on our scorching hot summer months.

The first distant view of snow was guzzling peaks of Himalayas seen from Darjeeling but as we always visited the hills in summer, this remained a distant chimera. The first time, I saw snow close up from within touching distance was while travelling with my wife in Himachal. Excited, we stopped the vehicle to mess with it, and found it wet, messy and not too clean.

Luckily, further up, there was fresher snow, in pristine white sheets covering the rolling slopes. What an invitation to act like the Bollywood couples and roll down the snow, singing, and throw snowballs. We immediately succumbed.

But then the practical difficulties became evident. It obviously was numbingly cold. Secondly it was wet. Thirdly, it hid rocks and bushes and frequently, horse dung and sheep droppings. Finally, it is very difficult to control the speed when you roll, and gravity makes you slide down at an alarming pace, in undignified positions, creating a mini avalanche as you go hurtling down, and are dumped unceremoniously in a heap at the bottom of the slope, wet, cold and dizzy.

I wonder how the Bollywood ladies did it with such panache, in skimpy clothes, smiling and singing all the while. We were bruised, out of breath, dishevelled and shivering, though bundled in jackets with hoods.

Snowball fights too were a letdown. If you hold the snow for a few extra moments in your palm, while you are shaping it into a ball and taking aim, it turns into ice. Therefore the missile when it hits you, hits like a rock. It doesn't elicit giggles or song, but yells, tears and swearwords, and can even draw blood. Another Bollywood myth busted.

Since that day, we have encountered snow numerous times, in all the Himalayan states of India, in Europe, North America and even in South Africa, and it has been beautiful, lovely, exciting, uncomfortable, threatening and even downright frightening. On two occasions, they were even life threatening.

The first view of snowfall was beautiful, and it melted on the skin. It was fun trying to catch it on your tongue. My little daughter was loving it. But soon, it came down heavily, obliterating the view, and covering the track, making it hazardous to walk. This was especially frightening as we were on the trek to Kedarnath, and I was carrying my five year old daughter on my back, and we were on the narrow steep track with a deep gorge on one side. A delay had made us late and the weather had suddenly turned vicious. I lost contact with the rest of my family, and visibility had reduced to a few feet. A strong wind started and turned this into a blizzard. I took shelter under a rock and was wondering how long we would last before freezing and trying my best to shelter my child and keep her dry.

Suddenly out of the gloom, loomed up, an angel of mercy, in the shape of a pack horse, and his owner. For an exorbitant sum, they agreed to take us to shelter. How our angel of mercy found footing and saw his way I will never know, but we were soon delivered to the rest house, less than half a kilometer away, to be reunited with my panicked family. If this lone horse and rider had not been delayed on the way and bumped into us in that narrow track, we might have conceivably frozen to death within shouting distance of help, given the weather.

As my kids grew up they tried sports in the snow, which alas I could never master despite sprains, bruises and frozen posteriors to show for my efforts, but next to the sea, snow was our favourite holiday destination.

We once again witnessed the might of snow during a road trip to Ladakh, near Druz, just after Zero point, on route to Kargil, where we proposed to stay at the army camp. A typical political trouble had delayed us enroute, and it was late afternoon when we crossed zero point. A shepherd warned us to turn back as the weather had turned foul. There were ominous dull booms we could hear. After waiting a while we decided to go ahead following some army trucks.

The view that awaited us was mind-blowing. An entire mountain of snow had descended on the road, taking everything in its path. We were witnessing an avalanche.

We were stranded, but along with dozens of other vehicles. Ultimately we were rescued by the army and spent the night in the camp, but that is another story.

Chapter 4
YAKS

Have you seen a yak?

Imagine a cow on steroids, wearing a shaggy fur coat that has seen better days and in urgent need of cleaning, and there you have it.

You bump into them, not literally, that would be scary, in the upper reaches of the Himalayas. Ladakh, Kinnaur, Spiti, North Sikkim, are places where one may meet them.

It is not a pleasant experience, as on top of the forbidding exterior, topped by two ferocious looking horns, they have a steely blank menacing and hypnotic gaze, which even Clint Eastwood cannot better.

They are said to be domesticated, but do not appear to be. Sometimes they are accompanied by Tibetan herders, who, except for the horns, don't look very different. The herders are a friendly lot, smiling at you, and provide shelter, tea, Maggie noodles and beer to visitors, for a hefty price.

Despite the size and looks, these creatures are Satvik vegetarians, and live frugally on the sparse grass and shrubs of these inhospitable climes. But they have another very nasty food habit, about which this tale I plan to tell.

We were trekking in Kinnaur in Himachal, and came across these scary beasts grazing calmly near our campsite. They made us all nervous, the ladies more vocally so. However, they kept in their place and we retired exhausted after a long tiring day and some cheery music around the campfire.

Trouble started next morning when we had to venture into nature to answer nature's call. As we looked for suitable shelter among the rocks and the few trees, downstream from the camp, (upstream being reserved for drinking and cooking water), we noticed to our dismay that these humongous yaks were dogging our footsteps like Mary's little lamb.

Imagine the scene. A nervous urban fellow carrying his paper roll or water bottle dodging between trees trying to shake off a huge shaggy pursuer with terrifying horns and dead pan eyes in the high Himalayas like a scene from a Hollywood spy thriller. Most of us returned with our morning business unfinished and looking terrified by the experience.

Consider the plight of the delicate city ladies who were terrified of cows in the first place. Being stalked by the

King Kong of the bovine world on the way to the toilet first thing in the morning was a trauma that would scar them forever.

The mystery was solved by the smiling herdsmen through our guide acting as an interpreter. Apparently these bovine mammoths, to escape the monotony of the grass and lichen, had developed a taste for the human byproduct, as a rare delicacy available only in the trekking season. And they were determined not to be deprived of this treat. Accordingly, they closely followed the movable food dispenser, which they knew, delivered without fail in the morning. We were reassured that these shaggy stalkers meant us no harm, and wanted only what we left behind.

Explanation notwithstanding, it took nerves of steel to relieve yourself with a giant hairy head topped by ferocious horns staring at you with a fixed baleful glare from the distance of a few feet.

We pleaded with our guide that in future our camps should be as far as possible from these friendly Tibetans and their gigantic pets.

Chapter 5

CITIES I HAVE LIVED IN AND LOVED

I grew up in Kolkata, which was Calcutta those days, then moved to Delhi for college. My working life started in Chennai or Madras as it was then called, then back to Delhi, Kolkata, Delhi, and finally to Mumbai. Over time, I have learnt to love these four metros I have lived in, with their very different flavours and quirky charms. I will try to share my impressions of these cities here.

If cities could be compared to women, this is the impression I gather.

Kolkata is the ageing courtesan, captivating in her youth, now sadly past, trying half-heartedly to hold on to her old glory, not quite succeeding, but barely concealing her heart of gold behind a faux haughty façade.

Delhi as the loud, brash, nouveau riche buxom Punjabi matron, busy gossiping, plotting intrigues, flashing her unearned wealth and power, but large hearted, full of life, living it up, boisterously enjoying all life has to offer as her due, and generously including all comers to her party.

Chennai the prissy orthodox disapproving Amma, keeping a strict lookout on her domain, with pursed lips and forbidding expression, lest anyone acts inappropriately. She is protective and feeds you healthy and filling meals.

Mumbai is an enigma. She is schizophrenic. Not sure whether she is the smart new age woman or the vociferous bai or the Parsee matriarch, she keeps switching roles, being many things to many people, but welcoming all in her tight claustrophobic sweaty sexy embrace, that absorbs you, never letting go, making you lose your original identity and becoming part of her progeny, a Mumbaikar.

First impressions of a visitor---- Kolkata and Mumbai, that of people, people, oh my god sooooo many people!!!!! Assuming you are arriving by train, whether to VT, now renamed CST in the greatest sex change operation in the world, or in Howrah, the sea of humanity overwhelms you. But in Kolkata, the Ganga immediately outside or in Mumbai, the sea a short distance away provides a relieving breath, reassuring you that you can come up for air.

If by air, both Kolkata and Mumbai scare you with the visions of the urban sprawl below, but reassure you with glimpses of the Ganga or the sea in between.

Delhi strikes you with the immense space and the threatening people, and you realize you have to battle to survive and capture those spaces, starting with the duel with the autowallahs

Flying to Delhi of course stuns you. The T3 beats the famed Changi of Singapore or many vaunted international airports, and the Airport metro outshines its counterparts in most metros in the world. No other Indian city boasts airports or metros that are comparable in luxury and efficiency. Even the drive to the city through the octopus flyovers and Chanakyapuri and Rajpath creates the necessary awe that the imperial capital must inspire in the native subjects.

Chennai scares you for another reason. For the first time in your own country you feel an alien. The language spoken, the signboards are all, well, Tamil to you, and getting directions is a nightmare. The shoddy airport doesn't help. The autos outside the station are as good at fleecing as their brethren in the Capital, but do so in an incomprehensible language.

So much for first impressions. Will continue with my further studies on getting directions, street food, morning sounds and making friends in the four cities. Ciao for now!

Chapter 6
TRAVELLING LIGHT

From my student days, I had got addicted to the pleasures of unplanned and impulsive travel without fixed itinerary and agenda. The mode of travel used to vary from local buses, general compartment in trains and hitch hiking, sometimes on the top of trucks. The top of the drivers' cabin in trucks is surprisingly roomy, and a grown man can sleep there if not afraid of falling.

When I got married, I was lucky enough to find a mate who shared my enthusiasm for backpacking, although the means of transport were confined to insides of vehicles rather than the roof. There was a small gap when our children were very young but soon they too got used to from an early age to the rigors and pleasures of travelling rough.

But the one essential rule for this kind of travel was that we travel light.

Subsequently, age, relative affluence, sloth and timidity combined to make our travel a more comfortable if less frequent phenomenon, but at least once a year we still try to do an exotic vacation to remote corners which involves some degree of trekking, camping or roughing it; and the kids on their own continue to seek adventure and travel the less travelled roads. The taste of this experience is a lifetime addiction.

Over time, the dictum of travelling light too has undergone moderation, and this is the story of how that started.

Earlier, our aim was that we should not carry more than what could easily fit in one rucksack, and be carried easily by me when walking long distances, and was easy to stow away on bus train or airplane. This was irrespective of whether I was alone or with my wife and kids. As the kids grew older, the rule changed to each person chooses what to pack, and carries it himself or herself. My solution was to have just one pair of jeans or shorts for the entire trip, which I would be wearing, and minimum spare clothes. For all of us, books took the space of clothes, till kindle and iPad simplified matters.

This was usually not a problem, and the only mishap that was common was getting wet and in Indian climes wet clothes dry up and don't kill you. Moreover, a windcheater with a hood keeps you dry in most inclement weather.

On this occasion, we were going to Vaishno Devi and further hilly areas in Jammu and a colleague and his family was accompanying us. As the four of us had just one rucksack with us and my colleague whose wife presumably did the packing was carrying two suitcases and two other bags, her husband kept berating her on her unnecessary luggage quoting us as an example of travelling light. The long suffering lady looked thunderous but held her peace.

Trouble struck when I tried to clamber on to the saddle of the sad looking pony who was to transport me uphill. After a terrible experience climbing up to Kedarnath earlier on foot with my daughter on my shoulder, I had decided that discretion was the better part of valour, and had hired a pony to transport me and my daughter to the top. As I tried to swing my leg over the horse with one foot in the stirrup, my long suffering ancient jeans and companion of many trips gave way at the seat with a heart rendering sound.

As I was not carrying a spare, I used the pony owners' shawl to cover my modesty and hunted for a tailor. Finally, I was sitting at a road side tailoring shop while my jeans were being repaired, wearing the tailor's lungi, while the rest of the party waited outside.

I could hear my friend's wife berating him on the handicaps of travelling light and justifying the size of their luggage.

Since then, I have always carried a spare pair of jeans or shorts whenever on a trip.

Chapter 7
GOING SOUTH

I was in my final year in the University. I had virtually dropped out, not attending classes, and doing everything else possible in those laissez faire days of Delhi University.

By a stroke of good fortune, a classmate, a minor Dada or Don at the University, had decided to mentor me not only in nefarious activities, but also, through his unique logic, persuaded me into taking a few competitive exams. He in fact paid the fees, as I had spent all my allowance in less productive activities, and even woke me up and dropped me to the exam centres. I will write about him in a separate story.

Having taken these exams without preparation and barely awake, I had little hope of clearing any. But I did get interview calls, but having previous experience of how I tend to offend the interviewers with my general appearance and attitude, I had no expectations. I was certain I was unemployable and that I would fail my exams too.

But on my return from a crazy adventure in a forest, about which I have written earlier, in Close encounters of the Wild Kind, I found an appointment letter waiting for me.

Receiving the appointment letter was a godsend. My concerns regarding a bleak future of unemployment and poverty being allayed, celebrations started on a serious note. The relevance of the final examinations thus becoming negligible, I gave up all pretence of studying.

My colourful friend, unconventional philosopher and extreme lifestyle guide, who, as I said earlier, was instrumental in getting me employed, was also selected by the same organisation, and posted to my hometown, Calcutta. I was posted to Madras as it was then known, in the Deep South.

The joining date was a few days after the final exams, and it was a two day journey across the length of the country by train. In order to avoid confrontation with my going to be disappointed parents, who wanted me to study further and prepare for the IAS, I decided to join first and inform them later.

Now that my creditworthiness was established, as I was about to become a class one officer in a government organisation with what seemed in their impoverished state a princely salary, I jointly with my friend threw a party involving crates of bliss which lasted through the weekend. This merged into another farewell party that our friends threw for us, and a few very hazy days later, my friends uploaded me, barely awake, on the South bound train along with my Spartan possessions in a rucksack.

When I finally woke up the train had reached the badlands of Chambal, and the deep gorges and ravines and steep banks took me straight to the stories of the Wild West that had fired my imagination as a schoolboy. The men around me had spectacular moustaches and colourful pugrees. The women wore brightly hued sarees with thick silver jewellery and veils pulled over their face. A number of men carried muskets. They spoke Hindi with an unfamiliar lilt.

Next morning I woke up to a new world. My co passengers had changed and everyone around was speaking in a strange incomprehensible guttural tongue. There also was an unusual smell, which I later identified as a mixture of coconut oil, jasmine and camphor. The women wore long skirts and had flowers in their hair. The men wore white lungis. The calls of "chai, garam chai" was replaced by "kaffee, kaffee". The vendors sold coffee, and tea was nowhere in sight. The breakfast or tiffin being served was in banana leaves, and newspapers in an unfamiliar script, and consisted of idlis, vadas and curd rice.

This was the first time that I had ventured South of the Vindiyas. It was almost like being in a new country. I could not communicate with my neighbours except through sign language.

Early next morning the train rolled into Madras. I was bewildered and lost in a sea of humanity whom I could not understand, and was being solicited by a mob of touts shouting "Hotel! Taxi!" and a string of incomprehensible words.

Suddenly out of the gloom there emerged a beacon of joy, in the shape of a man in white uniform and chauffeurs cap carrying a banner "Welcome Mr Mukherjee"

This completely unexpected angel of mercy guided me to a white Ambassador car, with white seat covers, which a very grimy boy, covered in two days worth of the dust of the nation, was afraid to soil. This scruffy untidy unwashed being in much stained tees was thus bourn regally to a hotel in Maylapore, my home to be for the next six months.

The novelty of being in a hotel, getting a wakeup call with tea served in the room along with the morning newspaper, proper meals served buffet style with plenty to eat in a proper restaurant, seemed like a dream, just out of my university hostel.

A telegram home informed my parents of my latest whereabouts and career choice. Two thousand kilometres protected me from their displeasure.

I got used to waking to the strains of ladies practicing Carnatik music in the neighbourhood, and the sound of temple bells. I got used to men in white with foreheads streaked with holy ash. I got used to demure women with jasmine in their hair. I got used to polite people in buses, who would not sit in a ladies seat even if it was empty, in sharp contrast to the uncouth louts in my earlier city.

I discovered a new country, the Deep South.

Chapter 8
MAPLESS IN MADRAS

Years ago, my wife and I, unencumbered and impoverished young couple then, had decided to backpack across South India. I had backpacked around North India earlier in my student days, mostly hitching rides or travelling ticketless. My wife too joined me in these adventures post marriage, but by more conventional and legal means of travel, although the most economical we could find. However, these were mostly restricted to the states nearer Delhi.

What we had not bargained for was the complete breakdown of communications, as Hindi was a dirty word in the south then, and English was limited only to the city of Madras, as it was then called.

We took an overnight bus from Chennai to Madurai after some difficulty, but once there, we were completely at sea. Managing with sign language, we took a rickshaw that took us around the temple city. We also had the most incredible and delicious breakfast of idlis, vadas, and filter coffee for three, including our guide cum rickshaw man, for a princely sum of rupees two. That night we left for the nearby hill station of Kodaikanal, the bus tickets having been organized by our incomprehensible guide.

Our adventures in Kodai would be another story.

On return to Madurai we tried to get a night bus to Kanyakumari, our next stop. A gentleman at the bus terminus spoke Hindi, and kindly procured some tickets for us and put us on a waiting bus. We thanked the Good Samaritan and dozed off. We were woken by a clamour, and found the conductor shouting something in Tamil, and the bus stationary in the middle of nowhere in a pitch dark night. On enquiry, an English speaking co passenger explained that this was a chartered bus from Madras to Kanyakumari, and apparently two extra passengers had got up at Madurai where they had stopped for dinner, and he wouldn't proceed till he identified them. I clarified that we were those two, and offered our tickets. This produced even more vociferous protests, and our interpreter explained that these were worthless paper, and he wanted us off the bus right there. I appealed that you cannot abandon strangers at midnight amongst paddy fields in nowhere land, and we could get off in the next town, but he wouldn't budge. I too became belligerent and challenged him to make me get off. The impasse was resolved by the friendly interpreter who made a deal that we pay the conductor some money, and get off at Kanyakumari, which was the next town. My screaming in English seemed to calm the conductor, and after some hard bargaining in sign language, cash changed hands, and we started again. I mentally abused the good Samaritan of Madurai in five languages.

We were next woken up at Kanyakumari, which was completely deserted and pitch dark, at about two in the morning, and the bus went off, as did the passengers who alighted there. We two were left quite literally in the dark, lost souls in what appeared to be a ghost town.

Hoisting our rucksacks, we stumbled along the empty road, the roar of waves telling us that we were on the beach road, where the Tamilnadu tourism guesthouse was, and we had booked a room over the phone from their counterpart in Kodaikanal, and been reassured by a prompt "No problem" from the booking clerk.

I actually bumped into a sign that said Tamilnadu tourism in English, a situation I thought happened only in slapstick comedies, but it was our beacon of hope.

The building it pointed to was in complete darkness, and there was a locked gate barring our entry. Being persuaded by the good lady not to try scaling the walls, our luck being what it was, to avoid spending the night in lockup, futilely trying to explain that we were bonafide guests, we tried a more conventional approach.

Our shouting had no result, but a guard from a nearby building came out, and we found that he was from the next door Kerala tourism, knew Hindi, and a back entrance to our destination. Guided by this helpful man, we entered through a service entrance, and started hammering on the firmly locked doors to the reception, proudly bearing a sign, "24 hours check in"

The awakened manager came out, and to all our queries, wagged his head, saying "No problem" reassuringly, but making no move to check us in.

Taking the help of the helpful guard, we understood that there were no bookings, and the only words in English he knew were "No problem". However, there were plenty of rooms available, and we had a lovely room with a sea view, and watched the sunrise from our window, as it was dawn by when things had been sorted out.

Chapter 9

COOPED UP IN KODAIKANAL

I had been telling the story of our backpacking trip in the South of India in my previous story. As promised, here is the story of our trip to Kodaikanal.

We took a local bus from Madurai and checked in at the Tamilnadu Tourism Guest House in Kodaikanal. The town is a very pretty picture post card sort of place and is spread over gentle green hills, surrounding clear lake, half covered in mist with deeply forested ranges framing the scene. It is a very romantic and isolated place, ideal for honeymooning couples and we spend the day walking, boating and just lazing around.

The food was of course South Indian and looking for a change of palate, we went for dinner to a Tibetan shack which was famous for its food and atmosphere among the backpacking community. Previous trekkers in the area had given us the heads up.

The one mistake we had made was discounting the winter of a South Indian hill station with the arrogance of Delhites, insisting that only madrasis would need a sweater here. However, the weather was chilly and dressed only in T-shirts and shorts, we were shivering with cold.

The shack was warm, the Thukpa and Momos hot and the warming effects of Chang, the Tibetan rice beer, soon made us quite cozy and comfortable. The company was genial, a mixture of local Tibetans and foreign backpackers. But soon, most of the customers left and we noticed that it had become quite dark outside. Kodaikanal, we were told is a town that sleeps early and there is no night life.

Worried about the long trip back to the Guest House in the dark and empty tracks, ill clad for the cold and wet weather, we hurried out. However, the early darkness was due to threatening rain clouds and soon a thunderstorm broke out making us scurry back into the warm shelter of the shack. Our Tibetan hosts were kind and asked us to stay by the stove till the worst of rain is over and even offered us a torch and plastic sheets to cover on our way back.

But the rain showed no signs of abating. We called the hotel from the phone and had our host explain in Tamil to the Reception that we needed a hotel taxi to come and pick us up, but we were told that no vehicle was available because of the weather. We next tried to call the taxi stand but received similar replies and also were told that some trees had fallen making it impossible for them to move out.

The only other customer in the place appeared to be a regular, a tall curiously dressed and very drunk European. We learnt that he was a German who was a permanent resident of Kodai and some kind of environmental activist. He had not spoken a word throughout the evening. The landlord suggested that we sleep there and got some blankets and put a few benches together. Not relishing the prospect at all we prepared to somehow pass the night. The lone guest had also silently left, huddled under an anorak.

Suddenly there was a honking outside, and peering out in the rain we saw the headlights of a vehicle and the dim outline of a long American car. With a big grin, our host told us that it's the mad German and his ancient Chevy.

"He will drop you back." Were the sweetest words we heard.

It was a crazy ride through a pitch black night in howling wind and pouring rain huddling in a rattling car driven by a dead drunk German who silently managed to take us to the safe haven of our hotel.

Throughout the entire journey, our knight in shining armour did not speak a word, and to this day we do not know the name of our strange benefactor.

Chapter 10
KOLKATA

If you are visiting Kolkata for the first time, you are probably coming by train, as I did, and arriving at Howrah station. The sight that greets you is a teeming multitude, reminiscent of a Mrinal Sen film, and it overwhelms you.

Now you encounter the serpentine queue for the taxi, and the argumentative Indian venting forth in vociferous Bengali. Daunted by the sight of the immobile traffic you remember the unsolicited advice of your garrulous co passengers on the train, and follow the signs and the bustling junta to the Ghats, to take the ferry across to the city proper. The bracing breeze and wide expanse of water revives you and you are ready to face the city of many epithets; Kipling's 'City of Dreadful nights, RGs Dying City, Grass's Show your Tongue, or La'pieres's City of Joy'.

The initial confusion with the cacophony of the crowds, the exasperating traffic, and the congested bewildering urban sprawl slowly gives way to its seductive charms.

The 'Bhadralok' gentry, soft spoken and mild mannered as long as you did not oppose their favourite football team, be it Brazil or Mohan Bagan, or political party, or dada as in Sourav, is a most helpful if rather voluble species, and will make you an honorary Calcatian. Of course, if you have learnt a few words of Bangla, and profess a liking for Bengali food, sweets and Rabindrasangeet, the city is yours.

The theatre scene is fabulous, and tickets for class acts are dirt-cheap. Ditto the music scene, whether Bangla or Hindustani classical. The street food is cheaper than anything other than the MPs canteen in the parliament, and it beats anything available anywhere in the country. Only Bangkok can compare in the variety and taste.

The office goer's pubs in Dharmatolla are budget and people friendly, and shared tables lead to bonding with all and sundry. There are peculiar treats to be had, like the Chinese breakfast bazaar at Dalhousie, exotic oriental cuisine in china town, Burmese dhabas, Armenian churches, Buddhist pagodas and Jewish Synagogues popping up in the most unexpected places. The crumbling imperial buildings of Dalhousie are architectural landmarks in sad disrepair, and the pseudo Gothic married to opulent oriental palaces in North Kolkata seem funny, heroic and tragic at the same time.

If cities could be compared to women, this is the impression I gather.

Kolkata is the ageing courtesan, captivating in her youth, now sadly past, trying half-heartedly to hold on to her old glory, not quite succeeding, but barely concealing her heart of gold behind a faux haughty facade. And you are madly in love with her.

This is why, Bengali or not, anyone who has lived in Kolkata for a while, becomes an honorary Kolkatan, and you can take him out of Kolkata, but cannot exorcise the Kolkata out of him.

Chapter 11
THE UNEXPLORED GOA

Goa is a state I visit often, as it was part of the territory I oversaw for my organization, and is a popular venue to hold conferences, and I personally love the scenery and ambience in this beautiful, laid back, touristy, beach bound state.

I usually stay in a hotel near the airport and as close to the beach as possible. But last time, I decided to see Goa a little more intimately, and accepted the invitation of a Goan colleague to go and stay in his village home and explore the countryside, avoiding the tourist beaches.

Accordingly, once the official business of launching a new scheme with the unavoidable meetings with the ministry, politicians, media, ad agencies, vendors et all was done and dusted, I checked out of the hotel, took an extended leave and moved to a different Goa.

The first thing you notice is the greenery. It's a vivid green backdrop dotted with cottages, some painted colourfully. It is also teeming with shrines, Hindu or Catholic, depending on the population concentration, but often mixed. The standard uniform dress code for men seemed to be checked shorts and bare chests ala Sallu

Bhai, which went with the weather, and loose shifts like nightdresses for the women. The ubiquitous vahana was the two wheeler; scooties and bikes, perfect for the narrow winding roads, which were often blocked by someone pruning their coconut tree or repairing something.

The populace in general appeared to be at leisure, lounging around in the universal uniform of shorts in some verandah like sheds which were everywhere. On enquiry I discovered that they were temple verandahs, an essential part of Konkan temple architecture, which also doubles as the meeting place, village hall, whatever, and is the centre of social and political life. There were groups of youngsters on bikes gathered around village squares, but these temple yards were by far the most popular places to congregate.

I think that the density of shrines per square mile or per capita must be the highest in Goa. Every family has a family deity. Every village has a village deity. Every mohalla has its own deity. In Catholic areas, the idols of the local Gods have been replaced by icons of Mary or various Saints or sometimes just a cross, but their practices remain largely unchanged. They still go on processions round the village as the deities of the earlier religion did before them, and like their predecessors, congregated on feast days. Just the days have changed; instead of on Dussera or Purnamasi, it's on various feast days.

Richer and usually Brahmin homes are built around a courtyard, with a Tulsi manch in its center. In equivalent Catholic homes, it has been replaced by a cross. Usually the village is divided into mohallas, each representing a separate caste based on profession. The house I was in, belonged to the leather workers area and their neighbours were the washer men. These were poorer areas, and the houses did not have interior courtyards, but a central all-purpose hall, for gathering, dining, entertaining and pooja, as a deity graced a niche here too. Bedrooms led off this central hall. My host, who had prospered financially, had built large cement double storied house but had kept the original plan intact, as I could see from the neighbouring cottages. The house was painted in bright colours, and was shared by the extended family.

There was also the family temple next to the house, which served the whole clan and also the mohalla of leather workers. The verandah was as usual doubling as a council room cum recreation area cum village hall. I had a chance to examine the temple carefully. Inside the garbhagriha, or sanctum sanctorum, were three deities, the chief with horse and sword, called Vishweshswara, or Lord of the world. He is the Kuldawat, or God of the clan. He had a companion and a second in command, and he sits on the earthen floor, not on the podium. He is called Nitkari, or the God of daily routine matters. Outside the temple, there is another God, who does not have a temple, but sits under a tree. He is called Rastroli. He is in charge of villagers who have moved out and all mundane prayers. Problems he cannot handle are referred to Nitkari, and he in turn only refers the most difficult cases to Kuldawat. All matters of family, births, deaths, marriages, acquiring new property, starting a new venture, planting of crops, harvesting all have to be necessarily referred to these deities and their permission and blessings sought. The first crop, or the first time anything new is being acquired, it is offered to the temple before taking it home. This applies to clan members anywhere in the world, so wedding invitation cards, postcards, photos of new cars etc. were stacked there. Everyone tries to visit the shrine at least once a year, whether they are in Mumbai, Kolkata, Lisbon, London, or Rio; cities with the highest expat Goan populations, in that order.

I understood that the Catholics did exactly the same, except that it was the family, clan or village patron Saint who ruled their lives.

There were also two beautiful examples of amity between sects that I came across.

The first was the temple of Jagreshwara, an incarnation of Lord Shiva. He does not have an icon, but is worshipped in the form of a flame. Originally he was in the open, but his popularity resulted in a temple being constructed. His feast day is the first Monday after Christmas, and his chief devotees and patrons are Catholic. Both communities worshipped him, as his efficacy in granting prayers was renowned, but the Catholics took the lead, and he was their clan God. His feast was celebrated by a morality play with a dose of humour, called Dando, where female roles are played by men. Mainly farmers seeking a bountiful harvest take part, and the procession is led by Catholics.

The other was the Satyanarain pooja in the village. In the morning, Hindus led the Choir in the Church, and led the prayers too, and in the afternoon the Catholic priest participated in the Pooja and he and his congregation stayed for the Prashad and the lunch.

Breakfast in a Goan village is freshly baked hot Pao, or buns, hard exterior and soft inside like French bread, with spicy lentils and veggies and hot sweet tea. The Pao is delivered by the village baker to all homes, as baking at home is now a thing of the past.

Lunch is rice and shell fish curry, and some small fish called Lepo, as well as dried shrimp sauce. In my honour a bigger fish called Morso and an even bigger one called Chonak was cooked, but these are festive fare.

Panas, or Jackfruit is popular, and an idli like dish called panas bhakri or jackfruit cake was served, a traditional dish fast disappearing. We also had some sour sweet dark blue berries called kanna, which are available wild.

The popular evening adda was at the Gadi, or village pub serving the country liquor Feni, made from both Cashewnut and Coconut, a clear strong liquid with a pungent smell which burns the throat.

There are lemongrass, roots, ginger and other flavours available, tempered with local herbs. In season you also get Urak, the fiery semi distilled version obtained in the first crop. You get it in small glasses and toss it in like Tequila.

Most villagers have moved to the city for work, and agriculture is largely an indulgence for home consumption. The coconut plantations are a valuable source of income. Another popular side income is letting off their homes to backpackers, at what to the locals is a fabulous rent, and to the tourist thinking in Dollars or Euro; dirt cheap. So the village scene is interspersed with scantily clad white skin and blond mops.

Locals rarely visit the beaches, except for religious festivals that require it, or unless they are involved in the tourist trade.

The area is also dotted with various crumbling forts no one seems to have heard about, and quite a few ancient temples, including a thousand year old stone structure lost in a forest. There are also many hidden waterfalls, a Sweetwater lake within hundred yards of the sea, and some secret coves and tiny beaches in scattered uninhabited islands approachable only by boat, which very few tourists are aware of.

My brief vacation in the other non-touristy Goa over, I returned to the grind in the maximum city, with a new outlook of my favourite holiday destination. A Different Goa.

Chapter 12
CHANGING OPINION

A few years back, we had gone for a family vacation to Kashmir.

We had the usual apprehension and perception of the area based on media coverage that most outsiders suffer from.

It did not help matters that the car sent to pick us up from the airport by the owner of the houseboat where we were planning to stay, was driven by a tall lean Kashmiri in black robes, skullcap, full flowing beard and a fierce scowl.

On top of it he seemed taciturn, giving monosyllabic replies to my enthusiastic queries. We learnt that he was to be our charioteer for the duration of our stay, taking us to various parts of the valley, and finally to Leh via Kargil. It was not a cheery thought.

Assurances by the houseboat owner, whom I knew from a previous visit, that our driver was known to him, a good student whose studies were interrupted by a tryst with militancy, didn't reassure us much.

When the driver wanted my visiting card to help prepare his bill for the coming Leh trip, I was further worried about disclosing my identity as a government employee, and therefore a prime target for abduction.

Next day, while driving into the countryside, the heavy troop deployment along the highway made it look like we were in a war zone, a constant reminder that we are not in a peaceful tourist destination.

Having covered this route earlier on a road trip with some friends, I kept trying to show off my knowledge to my family, which seemed to thaw our escort, and he too started his guide routine.

Following lunch at a place that served traditional meatballs and rice, where we were stared at as the only tourists eating there, he took us to a tea shop which he claimed served authentic Kahwa, and his country cousin tried to sell us the raw material for the same.

After escaping their clutches, conversation switched to food and beverages. He explained that the Wazwan we had in Srinagar was something meant only for weddings and feasts, and this meatball rice was more of a staple diet.

Similarly, the Kahwa was a rare treat, and the beverage of daily routine was Noon Chai, or salt tea, which seemed to be something like a cross between soup and the Tibetan butter tea, having a long and complicated method of preparation.

On enquiring where we could sample it, we were told it is not sold, but is always available in traditional homes. I quipped that therefore caging an invitation would be the only way we could sample it.

After thinking seriously for a while, he asked if we would like to sample it in his house. Taken aback, and too embarrassed to turn down the offer, I tried saying we would love to, but that we wouldn't like to trouble them, and needed to get back before dark. He brushed aside any objections and started speaking into his mobile phone in Kashmiri, which we couldn't follow. Then saying that it's all arranged, he veered off the highway into a narrow country road.

The idyllic scenery of rural Kashmir was lost on us, as the comforting sight of troops bristling with arms was no longer part of the landscape, making us really nervous. Soon, we parked outside a hamlet with crowded wooden houses and narrow dirt streets, where the car couldn't enter, and were bid to get off and continue on foot.

Terrified, but not knowing what to do, we meekly followed. Our mobile connections, not being BSNL, were useless outside Srinagar.

Our little procession soon drew a crowd of interested onlookers, all following us and chattering incomprehensibly. A fiercely bearded Mullah stopped us and quizzed our host for a while before letting us proceed. Visions of newspaper reports of missing tourists flashed in our minds.

Finally, we entered one of those wooden houses, went up some narrow stairs, and were bid to sit in a largish room with wall to wall carpeting, a few scattered pillows and no other furniture.

After a tense wait, the room filled up...... with a bevy of beautiful Kashmiri belles, and a gaggle of giggling children, looking like a poster for tourism. Our beaming driver and I were the only males in the room.

A variety of glasses were produced, and a large flask, Samovar, from which the salt tea was served with a flourish, accompanied by homemade bland biscuits. We conversed through our interpreter, and learnt that we were the first 'Indians' they have met, or in fact remember entering their village, except for security men on raids.

Many photographs were posed for, and the ladies were introduced as our host's extended family, consisting of sisters, cousins, sis-in-laws and their kids.

An hour and many cups of tea later, we returned unmolested to the car, again followed by an army of chattering children.

Darkness fell as we drove back, but it didn't seem ominous any more. We returned to the twinkling lights of Dal Lake, our firm opinion that all Kashmiris and all bearded Muslims are potential terrorists gone forever, as our ideas of women in Purdah being the norm in such societies completely changed.

We now came to understand that Atithi Dev Bhavah is a pan Indian concept, followed even by people who thought of us as aliens from India visiting their land.

Chapter 13
FOREST TALES

CLOSE ENCOUNTERS OF THE WILD KIND

The tourists spotted some movement in the grass and a flash of colour. Alerted by their excitement, the forest ranger focused his binoculars. To his alarm, he noticed some people hiding in the grass. The tourists' initial disappointment that it wasn't a big cat gave way to renewed excitement at witnessing the capture of some poachers at first hand. The ranger sent a wireless message to his colleagues, and soon a posse of guards started giving chase to the unauhtorised humans in the tiger reserve.

The interlopers being chased were actually four college kids, having an extraordinary and highly unlawful travel adventure. The fugitives were Ron from Shillong, the crazy guy who was game for anything; Desi from Mumbai, who was the wildlife expert and an extremely law abiding citizen until recently; Jo from Australia who was trying to travel the world on a bicycle; and myself, the originator of all such harebrained schemes.

It all started a few days back in Delhi, when we were planning to go backpacking in Goa, when Desi wanted to join us, to have an adventure before starting his career in government. He also had some camping gear. So we borrowed sleeping bags and backpacks and promising to show him the real India AND bring him back safely, we took off in the Bombay Mail. Being low on funds, we dispensed with buying tickets, and huddled on the floor of the general compartment, where the vast majority of my countrymen travel gratis, being too poor to buy tickets, and not much concerned with legalities. Few ticket checkers brave those crowds to catch offenders.

On the way, Desi spoke of the Ranthambore Tiger reserve, which he hadn't been to, and which was not far from Sawai Madhopur, a station we were passing through. So a toss of coin decided that we get off there, and continue our journey after a detour in this forest. From Sawai Madhopur, we hitched a lift on a tractor up to the village at Ranthambore. While waiting for a lift, we met Jo and his bicycle, with a fund of stories of cycling around the heart of India. Fascinated, we promptly co-opted him in our team, and dragged him along with us.

Utter disappointment awaited us at Ranthambore. There was no budget accommodation, and to enter the forest we needed a permit, which was available at Sawai Madhopur. Dejected, we decided to explore the ancient ruins and temple in the nearby hill and look for some food and shelter in the tiny hamlet there.

Here the warm embrace of Bharat awaited us. Not knowing the dialect, and Desi the only one with passable Hindi, we mimicked eating and sleeping to the ladies in all encompassing ghunghat, who seemed the only people there. We were invited into one of the homes, and fed what seemed to be large lumps of roasted dough with ghee and tall brass tumblers of buttermilk. This was my first introduction to the famed Dal Bati and Chach. The giggling ladies whose faces remained firmly behind veils found everything about us extremely amusing, our lack of appetite, when we couldn't consume the mountains of food offered, our not knowing the language, our seeking shelter in the village, and desire to explore the forest on foot. Falling over each other in laughter, they laid some charpoys in their courtyard and directed us to take a siesta, which we gratefully accepted.

Refreshed, we explored the ruins and visited the ancient temple, where a Rana was said to have offered his own head as a sacrifice to Shiva, and been suitably rewarded. We bathed and swam in the ancient tank by the temple, then got scared off by the resident turtles, which we took to be crocodiles, plenty of which we had seen by the lake.

In the evening, the men folk returned, and over communal chillums they promised to take us to the forest the next day, along with them when they go to illegally graze their cattle and collect firewood and other forest produce, which the law denies them but tradition promises them. Thrilled, we politely declined further hospitality, and went to sleep in the ruins, with many warnings from our hosts to never let the fire go out at night, or else.

So we decided to take turns to stay up and tend the fire, and ate bajre ka rotis and achar and gur which they had packed for us, made tea in Jo's billycan, without which all Australians are incomplete, and slept off in the deep silent forest, among ancient ruins where people offer heads to Gods, after sharing a companionable chillum. Jo's cycle was kept in the village.

We were woken up early in the morning by our hosts and strongly admonished, for we were all sleeping soundly, the fire was off, which was good, for only we could have been eaten by predators, but an untended fire can cause a forest fire and do untold damage. Duly chastened, we meekly followed them into the core area, in the spirit of civil disobedience. After a thrilling trek, where every bush seemed to hide lurking beasts, but spotting nothing more ominous than the herds of cheetal and neelgai, and packs of langoors and numerous birds, especially peacocks, we were escorted to a cave, said to be occupied by a sadhu, the sole human resident of the forest, who was to be our host that night, the villagers shared a meal and the communal chillum with us and left us rations of chana and gur, told us not to stray, stay out of sight, away from tourist jeep routes, animal paths, and forest guards, who in their view were more to be feared than the resident animals. We were also shown the escape route if spotted, as the guards had no jurisdiction outside the boundaries, and the nearest police station was Sawai Madhopur. Our offer of monetary compensation was turned down with hurt pride. We apologized and parted friends.

We bathed in the stream by the cave, and settled down in the coming dusk, waiting for the Sadhu in his cave, listening to the myriad forest sounds.

He came in silently, unsurprised by strangers in his abode, and taught us how to make rotis on bare rock among small flames, and curry from some wild roots and berries and the right way to fill, light and smoke a chillum. He spoke of his life and the reasons for this solitary life, his philosophy, the forest, and living in harmony. But that will be another story.

Thus started our second night in the forest, deep inside, but not pitch dark, as stars twinkled and moonlight filtered in through the trees, and not silent either, as the forest sounds from the stream, wind, trees and unseen creatures filled the night. The herbal stimuli were making our minds see animals at every shadow, and the unaccustomed diet was making my stomach rumble. Fear prevented me from moving out to the bushes to relieve the rumblings, and my companions prevented me from polluting the environment near the cave.

As to how this was resolved, and further encounters with wild animals and wilder guards, and how we survived to tell the tale, will come in episode two, as I am tired from typing and you from reading if in fact you have reached so far…

See you later, alligator, quite literally…..

LATER...

We left our hero, i.e. me, in a dilemma. This was resolved, quite literally, by a cliffhanger. I hung over the cliff outside the cave, clutching at vines for dear life, praying the tiger isn't about to pounce, and got rid of the excess Rajasthani hospitality that my delicate bong system was loathe to accept.

Early next morning, woken not by birdcalls but by screeching of langoors, we climbed down to the stream for a morning frolic, unaware of the import of the langoors' agitation. Soon the frantically gesticulating Sadhu called us back to the cave. There, he gently chided us for destroying the harmony of the forest. Apparently, the stream was part of the beat of a tigress, and the langoors were announcing the presence of her majesty. Unknown to us, but evident to the Sadhu, she had made a kill last night, and had enjoyed the meal at her favourite spot a short stroll away, and had been coming down to the pool for a refreshing drink, when our rude transgressions disturbed her majesty. The Queen of the forest had left in a huff, and withdrawn into deeper forest.

After a breakfast of Roti and Aloo courtesy our forest hermit, and tea courtesy Jo and his billycan, and enjoying our morning chillum and satsang, our host showed us the way to the lake via the stream, with a warning not to disturb the kill. Slightly skeptical, giving credit to the hallucinatory qualities of good jungle weed, we rounded the bend and stood still in shock! There, on a flat rock just below the overhang were the gory remains of a Sambar. We did not disturb the kill. It was the kill that deeply disturbed us. The pugmarks leaving the stream were clearly visible in the sand. They seemed very fresh. The thought that this kill could have been us, anytime that we were walking around this area, relieving myself late last night, or taking a dip this morning, when we were within sniffing distance of this mayhem made our hair stand on end. We hurried down the path, cursing Desi for having got us into this.

Further shock awaited us, but a beautiful one this time. In the tall grass, we came face to face with a majestic Sambar stag. We all froze for seconds, when suddenly someone breathed, and the magic was broken. The stag disappeared with a mighty leap.

We reached the ruins by the lake and found shelter, where we carefully lit a fire as the tourist lodge was on the opposite bank and we had to stay hidden. We dined on the villagers' gur and chana and Jo's porridge and settled down, taking turns to mind the fire and stand guard. Jo had been carrying a Lonely Planet, but blown away by this experience which no guide book had warned him of, he decided to donate the pages for rolling Js. After an incident free night we rose at dawn with the light shimmering on the lake and water birds everywhere. Herds of cheetal were at the lake, oblivious of us. As the sun rose, we saw some crocodile sunning themselves on the bank. This led to a problem as our water was being rationed for drinking only and we needed more for washing and for tea. We drew straws and I lost. With the billycan, a jerry can and a stick I went down quaking, stomping to make the crocks leave, as advised. They slithered off into the water. But the water near the edges was murky and covered in green scum, making it opaque. I was certain the prehistoric beasts are lurking just under, waiting to drag me down. Ignoring my friends' encouragements to go in and get clean water, I stood safely on the bank, as far from the water as possible. I hooked the billycan and jar on the stick and collected muddy water full of flotsam and vegetation. Jo patiently strained it through a cloth, boiled it and made tea, tricks he had learnt in the Great Australian Outback, and we had tea and porridge and left to explore the lake.

Finally our luck ran out. Some tourists mistook us for tigers, and disappointed on finding some kids instead, alerted the guards, and that's where the story began in Part 1.

Hearing the commotion and realizing that we are exposed, we stopped hiding in the grass, where we had crouched on the jeeps approach, and made a run for the fence, which was quite close here. We went to the tree our village friends had pointed out, whose branches straddled the fence and throwing our rucksacks over, climbed the tree and jumped the fence. The guards were still some hundred yards away.

Our great escape was being watched by a college bus trip waiting on the road outside. We whetted their curiosity, and Jo hurriedly collected his cycle from the villagers, whom we profusely thanked in broken Hindi. Then the students gave us a lift to Sawai Madhopur, providing a meal and transportation in exchange of our stories, much like the troubadours of old.

We decided to dispense with buying tickets again, much to Jo's delight, and decided to spend our remaining funds on a local brew called Santara. This was too potent for poor Desi, a teetotaler till then, but after the strain on the nerves he decided to sample some, and promptly passed out.

The first Delhi bound train that arrived was jam packed, and we just managed to get a foothold in a doorway pleading an ill companion and showing Desi. So space was made, the poor in our country being compassionate people, and Desi was stuffed between people's feet, while we sat on the steps of the open doorway. Jo used his skin colour to store his cycle in a first class compartment and came to join us. We spent the night perched on the moving train's steps, and occasionally pulling the comatose Desi out so that he could be sick on the tracks. We reached Delhi alive and returned to our Hostel and Jo to his backpackers' dorm.

I returned to find an appointment letter waiting, and have been serving that sentence since. Desi went on to top the Civils, and is a glamorous diplomat now. Ron lived our dreams, travelled the world, running canteens, gambling dens, being a tea taster despite drinking only alcohol, and is now settled in Europe. Jo, after a short stay in Delhi, cycled off in the sunset, never to be heard from since. We did not see the tiger on that trip, but much later. But for all of us, this was one incredible, wild, illegal, dangerous trip that we never should have undertaken, but are glad we did, because this experience can never be repeated or forgotten.

This trip obviously had no photographic evidence other than those seared in our minds.

Chapter 14

THE TIGER, I HAD COME TO THE CONCLUSION, WAS A MYTHICAL BEAST

Years of tramping up to its supposed haunt on days spent peering out of car windows, open jeeps, elephant backs and machans on freezing mornings, and even on foot (quite illegally of course) for four days and nights at Ranthambore (where you are supposed to trip on a tiger if you don't watch out and the beasts answer to their names), and not a sight. Cheetals aplenty, sambars, nilgais, barasingas and blackbucks, wild boars straight from the pages of Asterrix, all these were there. The tuskers in Corbett all knew me by sight and posed for photographs, but of the larger carnivores, not a sight. That is, if you don't consider the possible ear among the elephant grass, which could have bear a leaf or the thing like an ant near the horizon which disappears by the time the binoculars are focused or the sudden movement just beyond you when your co-passenger on the elephant or jeep screams 'tiger oye' and the mahout or guide glares at you.

Of course, there are signs in plenty. Pug marks dot the track as if a government sponsored canine rally it just over, droppings indicate severe epidemics of gas-tro-enteritis among the carnivores, left over kills hunt at orgies in open air, and the roars at night that could be 'Him' or a misfiring Maruti.

At Corbett and Sunderbans, Sariska and Ranthambore, Gorumara and Jaldapara, Periar and Rajaji, I drew similar blanks.

I was baffled by all this till the film 'Electric Moon' provided a clue. Thereafter I went on keeping a sharp eye for forest jeeps with pug mark tracks, hidden microphones in elephant grass and butcher's vans making delivery runs.

All this till Kanha happened. Falling for the spiel about kipling country from the attractive lady at the tourist office. We booked into the jungle lodge, at Kanha Tiger Reserve and took a slow train to Jabalpur. An interminable wait at the bus stop for the lone bus only to be told it won't make an appearance, and exorbitant and jarring marathon taxi ride, a jungle lodge disclaiming all knowledge of reservations, the power cuts and candle-lit dal roti, did not augur well for the trip.

The early morning jeep safari at Rs. 8 a km, our eyes firmly glued to the audiometer and the mind busy calculating the budget and cash balance (credit cards not having penetrated kipling country yet) kept our attention away from cheetal, pug marks, droppings, et al – till the second day.

It began well with a bull buffalo threatening us for photographing its cows, a barasingha with a bureaucratic reluctance to move and mon pug marks when finally hi-tech piped in. A wireless message to the effect that a big cat had been spotted on a kill made us rush to the nearest track and carry on from there on elephant back.

Suddenly, six feet from us, a sight that made all the trouble worthwhile – the Real Thing. A pair of tigers on a kill. Dissatisfied with the short glimpse after a long wait reminiscent of a 'darshan' of a deity and tipped off by a ranger that they will return to the kill, we returned the next day. For a handsome tip, our mahout let us stare uninterrupted for almost one hour at the gruesome sight of the feast.

Finally, the kill, or young buffalo was almost exhausted and a very brief battle for the spoils ensued, accompanied by roar, trumpeting elephants and screaming tourists.

The sudden commotion made me drop my camera and the unforgettable sight was captured only in the mind's eye in audiovisual splendour. For the roar of the free beast of six feet is something you cannot ever forget. The creature in the wild appears to be a completely different species from the sad specimens we see in our zoos and circuses.

I came back converted. The tiger is alive and roaring.

Chapter 15

ARANYER DIN RATRI.. DAYS AND NIGHTS IN THE FOREST

This was the title of Satyajit Ray's iconic film about a visit to the Santhal Parganas.

We were planning a similar trip to a forest eco resort in the area.

On hearing that the nearest railhead is Muri, I went back to another childhood memory, the Tenida classic Char Murti, where the adventure starts from Muri Station.

Watching the Kannada film Kantara, brought back the stories that I heard from the Santhal people we met there.

We were the only passengers to alight at the sleepy station at Muri and found no one waiting for us.

Someone from the homestay was supposed to pick us up.

This reminded me of Tenidas' adventures for they too found no one at the station and had to walk.

As the forest area didn't have internet coverage, we couldn't use Google maps, hence driving there was ruled out.

But the deserted station compound had a single vehicle parked there, and a man sleeping inside.

On being woken up he told us that he was our guide, more similarities with Char Murtir Avijan, where their guide had been taking a nap as well and missed the train.

Anyway he took us down narrow winding thickly forested tracks for an hour's drive to our destination, a scenic set of 5 cottages next to a lake, surrounded by hills and forests.

We walked, trekked, explored the waterfalls and villages, tried swimming in the lake and climbing the rocks.

Our driver for the next few days and all the employees at the resort were Santhals from a nearby village, which we also explored as their guests.

We were the only guests, and some government officials on a survey, staying in tents nearby, came for meals, as it was the only place serving meals in the area, if informed in advance.

Meals were rice, veggies grown there, fish from the lake or the stream next to it, free range chicken kept there, only the sweets being brought from the town and stored there.

They could also arrange for Mahua, the forest liquor popular with the tribals, and had musical instruments, which were a part of their lives, and promised us a full blast party once the other people left.

As a child I used to visit my grandparents' farm in winter, and made friends with his farmhand's children, many of them Santhal, and had visited their villages. I had also picked up a smattering of Santhali.

Santhals, Muslims, Kevat or fishermen, all tenant farmers, had separate villages.

I remembered many of their customs and a bit of the language and pestered our hosts trying to see what changes have occurred over 4 decades.

The Government Officials left next day, and the evening became a riot of music, dancing and Mahua, in which we participated in full, and my daughter, a skilled musician wowed them with her ability to pick up their instruments and tunes if not the words. They were even indulgent of my amateurish attempts, and invited us to their nightlong sessions in the villages, as it was Govardhan puja time, with 5 days of non-stop festivities, culminating in the pig sacrifice.

But I will write more about this later.

Here, I want to write about the changes I noted in their lifestyles, and some intriguing insights gained from their answers to my questions and stories shared by them.

I learnt that the Santhal language now had a script, and was taught in school.

A funny change I noticed was that instead of calling everyone by the familiar '*tu*' as earlier, which offended government, judicial and police officials, they now referred to everyone by the honorific '*aap*', including when referring to the pigs.

None of them had converted to Christianity, and there were no churches or missionaries, unlike their counterparts just across the border, and the reasons weren't clear. They were nominally Hindus, but actually worshipped the ancient spirit Gods or *bongas*, and had no temples, just thans, which could be a tree, grove, rock, cave or spring and totems in the villages. The mainstream Hindu Gods were incorporated in their religion, the names sometimes changed, and major Hindu festivals were celebrated, but in their own unique way, which basically involved feasting rather than fasting, music, dance, liquor, and animal sacrifice. The Vaishnava festival of Govardhan puja, one of their major festivals, which we witnessed, was celebrated in the same way, and the cows were worshipped with much dancing and singing. It culminated on Diwali, with a pig sacrifice.

I understood that Govardhan Puja comes after Diwali, but this is what my hosts explained, unless I misunderstood in translation.

Incidentally, the neighbourhood Christian tribes celebrated Xmas the same way, with chicken sacrifice and the songs just replacing their ancient spirit Gods with Jesus.

The ojha or shaman still ruled, and only for major diseases was the doctor consulted, but parallel treatment by the shaman continued without the doctor's knowledge.

Their main livelihood was cutting wood from the forests and selling it in the nearest towns, carrying it all the way. This is the only work that the men did.

The women did everything else, farming, fieldwork, animal husbandry, gathering forest produce, housework and even building the huts. We got to witness this as during the festival, homes are repaired, painted and decorated beautifully by the women, who even collected the materials from the forest.

The men also hunted, especially during the traditional hunting festival or Hool, which is still going strong despite being banned by the law.

They said that forest officials being government servants rarely visited the forests, and anyway didn't want to antagonize the people. Many were from the villages and secretly participated.

The police wanted bribes but only if you used the border posts they manned, which could be easily avoided.

The area was a Maoist stronghold and the army was stationed there for 10 years after the uprising was suppressed. The Naga battalion who were there, became good friends of the villagers and helped them in many ways including farming, and gave medical care, provisions and gave people lifts. They learnt Santhali and many villagers spoke Nagamese.

Nowadays they've been replaced by the CRPF, who are more aloof and threatening.

The earlier brief clothing has been replaced by western clothes for the men and younger women, and the older women wore saris but far more modestly.

The population was 90 % Santhal, but the men in power were Mahatos. As our driver explained, the tribals were simple people and dealing with cunning outsiders could only be done by the cleverer Mahatos.

The government had tried to settle Muslim immigrants from the neighbouring countries there, but the belligerent natives soon drove them out, and there were no Muslims outside the towns.

They still carried the ubiquitous axe, an essential part of their wardrobe, but nowadays left them and other arms like bows and arrows and spears at home when visiting the town or courts or government offices, as it scared the babus.

They also confessed that the animals have become scarce because of constant hunting, but it was their vocation and couldn't be stopped. This conflict has been shown in the film Kantara, based in Karnataka. I suppose the stories of indigenous forest dwellers are the same everywhere.

The musicians and dancers had visited different parts of India as part of the cultural troupe and interacted with folk artists from other cultures. The younger generation were literate and the village headman proudly told us that his granddaughter was the first post graduate from the area and worked as a nurse in the town.

The Maoists had disappeared but I felt that they had introduced the idea of their rights and political power to the people, and they were keenly conscious and proud of their identity. They were well aware and extremely proud that the latest president of India is from their community, the first tribal to hold the top post in our country, but said that they're keenly watching, whether she remains one of them or becomes an alien like all city people.

Chapter 16

DIVERSITY

Recently we had the privilege of witnessing a major religious festival of 2 very diverse and little known communities, both rarely experienced by outsiders.

Interestingly both are Vaishnava festivals, but couldn't be more different from each other.

The first was Govardhan puja, which happens just before Diwali, and is a pastoral festival of cow herders. I had earlier seen this celebrated in North India, and the roots are in an episode of Krishna's childhood.

But amongst the Santhals of Ajodhya hills, this is celebrated in a way that would be completely unrecognizable anywhere else and would shock traditional Vaishnavites.

They celebrate this in much the same way as they celebrate any other festival, even Christmas, by the converts.

They paint their houses and draw beautiful pictures, and decorate the village and their cattle, which are worshipped, in a song called gaijagani.

They dance to traditional folk music, to the heady beat of drums, imbibing freely country liquor brewed locally and feast on meat from sacrificed birds, whose colours are specified for various occasions. The pig is reserved for the final day, Diwali, when, like their Bengali neighbours, they worship Goddess Kali.

All the songs are not religious, and I heard a lot of satire and protest songs along with the more traditional ones.

Basically they continued their age old practice by which they worshipped their ancient spirit Gods, just changed the names around when they converted to mainstream Hinduism of the plains people, or Christianity of the missionaries.

The other was from further east, in the island of Majuli, the largest riverine island in the world, on the Brahmaputra, in Upper Assam.

This island can only be reached by boat, and has a unique Vaishnava culture, which has been largely preserved intact for more than three centuries, when Shankardev visited the island and established this as the centre of the new movement that he was propagating.

It was the reformation of medieval Hindu practices, which was largely Tantrik in the East, and he introduced Vaishnava culture to Assam, which continues to be the primary religious practice today.

He was a multifaceted personality, and wrote songs and plays on Krishna's life, setting them to music, and choreographed dances, introduced mask making and established a series of monasteries which would preserve and propagate these art forms as a method of spreading the Krishna cult.

We were lucky to visit during the festival of Raas, when each village puts up a grand show, a re-enactment of Krishna's life, but in the exact same words and to the same music and choreography as originally created by Sankar Dev, 350 years ago.

The performances go on all night, and are repeated 3 days in a row to full houses. The same show every year with the same words, tunes and gestures doesn't pall on the audience. The star is the villain, Kamsa, whose larger than life performance enthrals the audience.

All villagers are teetotallers and vegetarian during this period, and elaborate meals are cooked. Fish however, is considered a vegetable here, as inevitable in an island community.

The performers are all local people, but the standards are extremely high. The audience comes dressed in finery and are vocally appreciative.

This unique eco system is now preserved as a United Nations cultural heritage but the credit for preservation goes to the monasteries and the local population.

The dance form introduced by Sankar Dev is the only classical dance form in Assam and has nuances of Kathak and Manipuri.

What astounded me was that a miniscule agrarian community cut off from the mainland adopted the teachings of a reformer from distant lands and preserved intact this culture for centuries, and have made it known around the area and slowly gaining global recognition.

We returned enriched, despite the language barriers, as the story was familiar, and the root language is Sanskrit, thus many words were quite similar to North Indian languages.

I was left wondering about the diversity of our country, where the same Religion is practiced in two neighbouring states, both festivals based on the stories of Krishna's childhood, in such dramatically different ways as to be unrecognizable as being part of the same religion.

This is the personification of the cliche... 'unity in diversity'.

Chapter 17
THE GATEKEEPER POET

We were exploring a lesser known part of our country, Upper Assam, and trying to understand a little known part of our history, the Ahom dynasty that defeated the mighty moguls, which somehow has been ignored by our academics, and the classical Vaishnava sub culture, unique to the region and quite unknown outside.

But more of that later.

This story is about our accidental interaction with an unusual guide to Ahom Palace near Shivsagar.

We had declined the services of the guide kindly provided by the local administration, in order to explore at our own pace, and avoided the usual throng of half informed rapacious guides as they are usually a nuisance, but later regretted as what we saw didn't match with what we had read up.

It was then that suddenly a security guard loomed up, toting an AK47, and asked in broken Hindi if could he explain?

He proceeded to give us an erudite lyrical and passionate presentation on the Palace and it's history leading up to the current times of the ULFA using the place as a tactical HQ, the army flushing them out and sealing the underground passages, and the earlier rapacious degradation by the English searching for hidden treasures, the later neglect by the powers that be, and subsequent takeover by ASI, when only the shell remained.

He explained the intricate defences, optical illusions to detect infiltration, and the thrilling history, bringing the ruins to life.

My wife joked that I'd better pay him whatever he wanted, as he carried a gun. But he was very reluctant to accept a tip as he said that it was his passion, as he was an Ahom, perhaps a descendant of this forgotten kingdom, and that he was a writer, poet and musician by vocation. His passion did not pay for his sustainability, so he worked as a security guard and followed his heart writing poetry, history and fiction, and self publishing.

He had spent almost three decades with the BSF, fighting terrorists and our neighbouring enemies in Kashmir, Jharkhand, Rajasthan, Punjab, and the North East. He had to keep his passion for the arts a secret, and on retirement, had become a security guard to give himself time for his first love, poetry, music, literature and history.

He proceeded to regale us with his music and lyrics, and refused any monetary compensation, saying that all he wanted was an interested audience.

He returned to his duties leaving us all the richer for the unusual interaction with the poet gatekeeper.

Chapter 18

THE INTERNATIONAL ADDA IN SKY

In the days of old, Serai on the major highways of the World like the Silk Route and our grand trunk road were locations for meeting of minds of an exotic variety of races, cultures and communities aided by the spirits of distant lands. Place names ending in Serai or Inn like Sheikh Serai, bear witness to this.

Nowadays, this international meeting of minds and feasting of souls aided by exotic spirits has moved upwards to the skies to the bars on the business class of international flights.

Flights to the business hubs of the world from India are all long haul and usually overnight. Flights also induce insomnia, especially when you are changing time zones. Moreover, it is deeply ingrained in our psyche to get the money's worth for our tickets by guzzling as much of the free booze as possible.

Thus we find an international collection of insomniacs, drunkards, freeloaders, and globe trotters congregating in the bar in the sky. They are usually regaling the captive audience of the stewardesses manning the bar with stale jokes in various accents or boring stories of business triumphs and wealth acquired, much like Othello tried to woo the fair damsel with stories of Valour and Glory.

However, it gives us a chance to meet people from countries you cannot find on the map and learn about cultures we have little or wrong knowledge about.

People from our western neighbour whom we love to hate turn out to be quite lovable especially after you have shared a few large ones, which you thought were haram for them. As it turns out such dictates are followed only on paper. They speak the same Punjabi that we do, crack the same jokes, are as irreverent about their political and religious leaders and drool over the same Bollywood starlets that we do. We only differ in the cricket teams we support. During one such encounter, Mr. Khan from Lahore ended up inviting me for an all paid holiday in his country and I extended the same welcome to him, knowing fully well that we will soon lose the cards exchanged and never really stay in touch or take up the offers, but perhaps someday, inshallah ……..

Then once there was this lady from the tiniest country in the world tucked into a corner of Switzerland which we could not find in the map nor could we spell or even pronounce after having imbibed freely of the spirit that cheers. All I remember is that the country began with an L, and the lady told the most improper jokes about various nationalities of Europe she had encountered.

There was another lady from Cyprus and I learned that they too have a story very similar to our Kashmir, and she was bitter about her parents having to flee their homes when Cyprus was divided in two. She remembered the exact date. They call the other portion occupied Cyprus and insist that it is part of their country. But Turkey calls that portion of Cyprus a district of Turkey. The split was on religious grounds when the Christians had to flee the occupied portions which were resettled by Turkish immigrants, thus, changing the cultural character and even language of that part. She was strongly Islamophobic and anti-immigrant. There was a Cypriot film in the Airlines collection which talked about the border and bonhomie between the Cypriots of both sides cantered on a dog which crossed the border. She disregarded the film as liberal nonsense and said that she hated the occupiers with all her heart.

Arabs from the Middle East did not look anything like Lawrence of Arabia and wore normal Jeans and T-shirts, were jolly cosmopolitan people who can drink us under the table and are well informed about global issues. Nor do they flout diamond watches or gold toothpicks. Another stereo type shattered. The only disconcerting habit was that they tend to hug you when parting after an hour's companionable drinking when a simple hand shake would have sufficed.

I received invitations to Cyprus, Estonia, Lesotho and the unpronounceable country with L, and in turn invited them all to India fully confident that we will never meet again but one co-barfly in the sky broke this stereotype.

Singh pra ji from sadda Canada, originally from sadda Punjab, after thirty two years in Canada, had not lost an inch of his Punjabiyat. He spoke a rustic dialect of Punjabi, even I had difficulty deciphering. And he actually lived up to his sozzled promise which I had completely forgotten, turning up at my hotel, taking me home, and giving me a guided tour of the area and generously playing host. We continue to be in touch through whatsapp.

Some bar in air friendships do last.

Chapter 19

JAMBO .... WELCOME TO THE ENDLESS GRASSLANDS

Serengeti, a Masai word meaning endless grasslands, was a place that had called out to me since childhood having seen the films Hatari and African Safari and read the book Mountain of the Moon. This had been reinforced by the National Geographic Visuals of the great animal migration from Serengeti in Tanzania to Masai Mara in Kenya and the journey back. At long last my dream was about to come true as we had booked a flight on Rwanda Airlines to Kigali, across the border from Tanzania and then a small plane to Arusha, the nearest Airport to Serengeti.

However, travelling in Africa is never that simple. We learnt in Rwanda that the flight had been cancelled and we were offered visa and hospitality in that country with the hope of a flight next day. We firmly declined and was given an option of flying to Nairobi in Kenya and try to catch another small plane to our destination. Desperate, we took that. After a great deal of tension at Nairobi, where my name had disappeared from their records, we finally got a flight to Kilimanjaro and drove to our destination from there with a night halt at Lake Myanara.

Our first welcome to Africa was at the wildlife lodge at Myanara when a troop of baboons (incidentally a group of baboons is called a Congress, but to avoid being mistaken for a political piece, I will refrain from calling them by their rightful name) invaded our room and grabbed the snacks and toiletry and started inspecting our luggage. Baboons being larger than dogs, with ferocious faces and huge canines gave us the fright of our lives and I had to reluctantly play the macho male and try to shoo them out. They did leave only to enter our children's room by sliding open the glass windows. Now my daughters joined the fray and proved that the young ladies of today are more than a match for the most aggressive African Ape. Perhaps averting unwanted attention from the Indian male is sufficient training.

The baboons left, and we felt that our children's clothes were arranged better from their attention. They also discarded the sunscreen lotion purloined from the room but ate up the biscuits and chocolates while posing for photographs. We realized that we are in Africa.

That day, we drove on through the Ngorang Ngora highlands and into the Savannah, where the great animal migration was gathering steam.

We encountered thousands of herbivores from the gigantic giraffe to the diminutive diki diki, the ubiquitous gnu, the spectacular zebra, six types of antelopes and dozens of predators from the mighty Simba the Lion, the sinuous Chuhi the leopard, the slinky Hyenas and the jackals which followed this bonanza of meat on the hoof.

But that story will be told by and by. I will complete the story speaking about our journey back. On the way back, we were flying from Kilimanjaro to Mumbai via Rwanda. However, we discovered to our horror that during the earlier rescheduling, the tickets to Mumbai had been cancelled and once more we were fated to be guests of Rwanda. Many protests and display of the original tickets later, they did issue us fresh tickets to Mumbai but told us to get the Boarding Pass at Rwanda.

On arrival at Kigali in Rwanda, we were told that our flight for Mumbai had left the previous day. Mystery was solved when we realized that the fresh tickets were booked at Kilimanjaro late night on the previous day but we arrived in Rwanda around midnight when the date had changed. On explaining the physical difficulty of leaving Rwanda before arriving there, they offered a solution – another flight to Mumbai via Uganda.

African airlines are a Kafkaesque world. Where when and how a flight would go is a matter of chance. And whether your name figures on it or only some of the names in the group is anybody's guess. Boarding tickets to destination x does not ensure that you board or that you go to that destination. And the time is completely fluid. Various officials involved have various opinions and none agree with what's displayed on the board or mentioned in the tickets. You learn fatalism in Africa. I have seen 4 countries for the price of one. Now waiting patiently to see where they will take us next and when.

We finally came back to India with indelible memories of Africa and forgettable memories of their Airlines although we did see four countries for the price of one, even if it was only the Airports.

Chapter 20
MASAI

To continue with my African Safari, this time I will talk about the dominant species, in most aggressive ape i.e. the homo sapiens. I will talk about the fascinating people of Tanzania, especially the largest group, the Masai.

The first Tanzanian Citizen, we got to know closely was our guide, a large, genial and extremely knowledgeable gentleman of the Chagga tribe who hail from the upper reaches of Kilimanjaro. He was earlier guide to the climbers to the Kilimanjaro and had started free lancing as a Safari guide some years back. He was a fund of knowledge not only on the Flora and Fauna of Tanzania but on the sociology, politics, geology, history and economics of the country as well. We learnt that Tanzania was a German Colony and was active in animal conservation even before independence. It also is the only African country with no history of Tribal warfare despite the large number of tribes sharing the country. What was even more extraordinary is that although there are two major religions, the Muslims on the coast and in Zanzibar and the Christians in the

Hinterland, there has been absolute communal amity. Inter faith marriage was common and the children could decide on either faith once they came of age. We actually met one such couple with their two lovely daughters Yashmin and Elizabeth.

We also learnt that the staple diet of the Chaggas was the Banana which grows in plenty around the Kilimanjaro and their favorite drink is banana wine which did not suit my palate.

But by far, the most fascinating tribe who constitute the largest section of the population are the Masai. Their language, Swahili is the official language of both Tanzania and Kenya and is widely spoken across central Africa. The Masai are nomadic herders who have chosen to maintain their lifestyle and culture over the centuries with the modern world making only peripheral impact on their lifestyles.

We visited a Masai village. Our guide knew someone there. A contribution of US$ 50/- had to be made to the welfare fund and we were given a traditional welcome by a party of warriors and a group of ladies with a dance and we were invited to join them and compete in a sort of Masai dance off. Of course we were thoroughly beaten by the very athletic warriors who were very amused by my efforts.

We were taken around the village and inside a hut and to their kindergarten, craft shop, and to meet the village elders and the Chief i.e. the usual tourist traps.

But what I found fascinating was that till this date, they have firmly stuck to their ancient lifestyle subsisting on a diet of meat, milk and blood only, all of which is the product of their cattle. They do not have any fruits, vegetables, salt, sugar or spices and no grains either and yet they maintain a fantastic physique. An advertisement for the Atkins diet perhaps.

Every warrior is dressed in a single red sheet and every one carries a machete, a club and a stick. The women are also dressed in a single sheet and wear beads around the neck. The social hierarchy is very strict and the Chiefs' word is Law. The Chief is selected on the basis of number of cows and number of wives. The average price of a healthy wife is fifty cows. Marriages are often arranged before even the birth of the children and no one dares protest. Our village was very small and the Chief had merely five wives and 100 cattle. Wives and cattle are both clearly in the possessions of the male and have less rights than domestic animals in other parts of the world. But both are well cared for as they are producers. The women do all the work including building their huts.

These huts are more like temporary nests or a single, small thatch of sticks covered with mud with a small low opening in one side and a smaller opening on the top for letting the smoke out. There is a fire at the center of the hut and place by the side for the man and one wife to sleep while another smaller area for the smaller children to sleep in. It is dark inside and at most 4 -5 people can enter at one time if they crouch. These huts don't last much more than a year and by then the village moves to the next pasture.

The load is carried by the women and the cattle and the trading is also done by the women. The sole job of the men is to graze the cattle and guard them from predators. You can see them standing on one leg balancing on the stick staring into space. A good life, no doubt.

The hospitality of the Masai includes a stay in one of their huts along with the attentions of one of the wives of the host.

Earlier, to reach manhood, they had to kill a lion but that has been stopped now and they can only kill predators if they attack the cattle. However, the fear of a Masai

Warrior is so high that the sound of the cattle bell prompts the predators to move away and leave the easy prey alone. The usual prey of the lions, the antelope and the zebra graze peacefully with the Masai cattle and the Masai do not harm any other animal. In fact, they live so much in tune with nature that they have been allowed to move freely within the game reserves and national parks without any permit, the only exception being Serengeti.

The power of the Chiefs can be seen from the fact that once the eleven Chiefs of that 14000 sq. km made an agreement with the Government, 60 lakh Masai peacefully left the area to the animals and not a single protest was heard.

In exchange, they are allowed to move and camp anywhere they like in the rest of Tanzania. They are largely illiterate and prefer not to send their children to school so that they are not tempted to leave the traditional life. The few who venture out and sample the modern world outside also often come back to their clan and village and revert to the primitive life style. Those who want to adopt a different lifestyle and marry partners of their own choice are allowed to leave the clan and marry into other tribes.

The Masai have their own religion and have not converted to either Christianity or Islam but some inroads are being made as we saw Madrasas set up especially for the Masais in the small towns which offer Dollars and a modern lifestyle in exchange for their souls, having limited success unlike the Christian missionaries who had tried this earlier.

Despite being the majority population, there have been no Masai Presidents so far but the Chiefs have a great deal of clout. The biggest Chief in that area had 50 wives, a few hundred children and a thousand head of cattle.

The only concession to modernity was the cell phones by which the warriors stay in touch with the village. We did meet a few Masai ladies who were working as waitresses at a Resort but even they were not sure whether they could escape the traditional life or would have to go back to the clan at the orders of the Chief.

The village money is used to buy water, cloth and iron, the only things they need from the outside world. They also buy and sometimes steal cattle from the other tribes as they believe all cattle belong to Masai and the other tribes, who were hunter gatherers earlier, can eat other animals whom the Masai don't touch.

The only people more exotic than the Masai were the Bushmen who are a minuscule minority. We, unfortunately, couldn't visit their village due to time constraint.

The other tribe whom the locals called Indian are actually Gujaratis and as we are quite familiar with them here, I shall not dwell upon this exotic fauna. But be prepared to be greeted with Kem Cho by the Africans you meet just as we did and be prepared for the surprise that you don't speak 'Indians' if you do not know Gujarati.

Next time, we will talk about the real denizens of the Savannah, the migrating beasts and their predators.

Chapter 21
THE LODGE

The lodge was a circle of cottages in a clearing in the savannah, perfectly blending in with the surroundings, with rocky outcrops, trees and grassland in between, a viewing platform with a spectacular view of the grasslands from where we could witness extraordinary sunsets and sunrises, which looked straight out of a Hollywood African drama.

The property was not fenced, and we were told not to venture out at night as animals strolled around, and a lion was seen relaxing in the gazebo just outside the bar. Perhaps it wanted a change of menu. As we had seen a kill just outside the gate, we were careful not to become part of the dietary options.

The place was overrun by Hyrax, Civet cats, Mongoose and Meerkats, so that the exotic wildlife of Africa was actually at our doorstep. As darkness descended, we were serenaded by the maniacal "woooah" laugh of the Hyenas, which continued all night, occasionally interspersed by the deep bass roar of the lion, presumably the family we encountered near the gate. But the interesting encounter was on the way back from dinner.

We usually cut across the lawn at the center, saving time and enjoying the excitement of spotting animals in torchlight. The Hyenas' howls we disregarded as we were told that they will run off as we approach, but there was a loud grunt. The kids assumed that it was a warthog, and were excited to meet Poomba now that Timon was all around. But the resort manager was frantically waving at us to stay off the lawns. As we made our way along the verandah, he explained that there was a hippo pool just outside, and at night the hippos come out to graze, which was what we heard, and though herbivorous, the multi ton monster with teeth yards long is the last thing you want to bump into at night. We did see her early next morning, waddling back to the pool, and her skin was a surprising pink. Hippos sweat reddish sweat when out of water, and when not caked in mud, has fairly light skin.

Next day we spent gazing at the bathing beauties skinny dipping in the Hippo pool, and witnessed some altercations between irate husbands jealously guarding their harem and sly Casanovas trying to make out with these substantial matrons. It was a fearsome display of gaping jaws and massive canines accompanied by grunts and splashes, but no actual violence. We also saw the crocodiles slinking past and keeping a safe distance from these mammoths.

On the way back we came across a fresh kill, but this one had a large pride and emancipated lionesses. A zebra was being devoured by eight hungry lions, and the pulling and tearing made the carcass jerk around as if alive. The beasts had torn the belly and were immersing their entire heads inside to get at the juicy organs, and their faces and heads were covered with blood, which they then proceeded to lick off each other's faces. It was a gruesome sight. We noticed that the lord and master was missing, and had been told that he gets dibs on the kill first, although the ladies do the actual hunting. We were told that this pride had been hungry for a while, and didn't want to wait for the boss, but eat up the best parts before papa arrives. Lionesses lib at work I thought.

We also spotted herds of Buffalo and Elephants, thus four of the big five were ticked off, and the rhino wasn't around, so we spent a whole day looking for the elusive Cheetah, of whom very few survived.

Their territory was different, as were their prey, and they avoided territories of the larger predators. But a whole day of driving around the never ending grasslands and peering at the sparse umbrella acacias yielded no results. We did find another elusive creature, the tree lion; who is nothing but a standard lion with a penchant for climbing trees.

She was sleeping peacefully on a low tree, and our truck parked directly below did not disturb her equanimity. But seeing a lion, even a sleeping one, about six feet away and just above our head height from an open truck, especially after seeing her sisters at the feast, was quite eerie. She briefly opened her eyes, pricked up her ears, sniffed slightly, tilting her head on one side, as if inspecting some goods at a shop and finding them wanting, went back to sleep.

After three days in Serengeti, the next day we moved on to Ngorang Ngora, where we were staying for the next two days, and will tell the story in the concluding episode.

Chapter 22
NGORANG NGORA

The final part of our African safari..

The last two days of our stay in Tanzania we decided to spend in a unique ecosystem, the crater of an extinct volcano Ngorang ngora which is a sunken bowl shaped valley surrounded by high ridges on all sides. The rich mineral land makes the vegetation lush and green throughout the year. It is fed by streams flowing into the crater and water supply is all year round. Thus it happened that animals that wandered into the crater never left. Stray elements from the great migration of Serengeti have been moving in and flourishing in the valley. As a result it has the highest density of wildlife anywhere on the planet.

The name Ngorang Ngora came from the sound of the cowbells of the Masai herds who grazed their cattle in the valley. Of late the Masai have been persuaded not to graze their cattle inside the crater.

We stayed at a lodge on the rim and through binoculars, could spot the rich fauna in the valley. Immediately on arrival we hit pay dirt and spotted the only member of the big five that was not present in Serengeti. There was a group of rhinos by the lake in the middle of the crater.

We were lucky to witness an exciting drama of animal life. A mother rhino and her calf were strolling along and a lion was stalking the calf. The calf noticed and squealed in alarm. The mother noticed, turned around, saw the lion and started a lumbering charge. The lion knew when it was beaten and scampered off. The rhino collected the calf and disappeared in the shrubbery.

The next day we descended into the crater. The first sight that greeted us was a perfect example of the food chain.

A gnu was being devoured by a pack of lions, one of the seven prides that reigned over the crater, dividing the territory between them. Keeping a respectful distance around them was a ring of hyenas, waiting their turn. Short distance further back was a circle of jackals waiting patiently. On a nearby tree, waiting impatiently and occasionally hopping down was a pack of vultures to feed on whatever scraps remained.

When we returned that way in the evening there was not a scrap of bone or skin to be seen, as if the feast had never happened. Only a solitary satiated hyena was dozing in the grass and lazily lifted it's head to observe us.

During the day we drove around the crater basin spotting all the fauna of Tanzania at frequent intervals till we were actually getting quite used to it. We did spot more rhinos but they ignored us. The cheetahs remained elusive unfortunately. We spotted six of the seven prides of lions during the day, and the seventh we saw in dramatic circumstances at dusk which I will relate now.

While we were on the road back to the lodge at dusk a further drama awaited us.

As we were entering the wooded area there was a huge commotion. A number of elephants were trumpeting simultaneously. We saw a herd of elephants stampeding and apparently running around in circles quite close to us. It was a terrifying sight.

We stood still and watched the drama unfold. The elephants made a circle with the adults facing outwards and the calves kept in the centre. Our guide explained that a pride of lions had been stalking the herd trying to isolate and kill a straggling calf. The calf noticed and raised an alarm and the herd took a defensive position.

Once the calves were secure the tusker charged the lions, scattering and driving them away.

It was a spectacular climax to our African safari.

Chapter 23

CAPE TOWN, THE DARK SIDE

Once, I had the opportunity to visit Cape Town in South Africa for a Conference. I was very excited as I recently had an extremely memorable vacation in that Continent at Serengeti in Tanzania in East Africa. Moreover, Cape Town is reputed to be the most beautiful City in the World.

On the drive to the Conference venue from the airport and the evening drive around the Town, and especially the water front, this was quite evident. The majestic table mountain in the backdrop, the gently rolling hills, the vivid blue sky, the verdant green fields, lush greenery everywhere, the azure sea never far from the sight, spotlessly clean streets, beautiful buildings, it seems like a film set and not real world at all.

As we discovered, it was a film set, and not the real world at all. The curtains were lifted, thanks to our articulate and politically aware driver, who was a Xhosa. He pointed out that the beautiful neighbourhoods we were going gaga over were all exclusively white, while the black Africans lived in townships which were horrendous slums and dens of poverty, crime, vice and drugs and no white man dare enter those neighbourhoods. These slums too were divided according to tribes and coloured or mix race people and Indians had separate townships or ghettos. He also informed us that when a few rich Indians purchased property in a white neighbourhood from some impecunious liberal white at a good price, this started a stampede of whites from the area, making property values fall and prices in the countryside to soar as whites flocked to the fully white farmlands.

He also pointed out that all Executive Level jobs in the hotels we were staying in and the companies we were meeting were held by white people irrespective of educational qualification and all the menial jobs are done by the native black population.

I observed that this was true and all the delegates of colour were from the other African countries whereas the South African company representatives were Lily White, as were the managerial staff at the hotel where we were staying. But the security, housekeeping and restaurant staff were largely Xhosa or coloured. Incidentally coloured is a term for mixed race population of South Africa.

Our friend next made a few even more outlandish claims. He said that there would be no black people in a white restaurant, white shop or white school except for the staff and there would be absolutely no white faces in a black restaurant, black shop or a black school. When we expressed disbelief, he bet his fare for the entire day if we could spot an exception while he drove us around. Eager to prove him wrong and possibly save some money, we tried to spot such anomalies but the black face we saw in the white café was a waiter; in the shop, a security guard; and the dash of colour in the white school was the gardener. In the similar establishments in the black neighbourhoods, there was not a single white face in any role whatsoever.

We also noticed that the white neighbourhoods, all had high boundary walls with barb wire over them connected to power lines. We were told that the wires are electrified at nights. We could also see signs saying 'beware of dogs'. 'Trespassers will be shot' and other such dire warnings. Our Xhosa guide told us that intruders from the townships are often shot while trying to rob a few fruits from these well-guarded gardens and the murderers get away claiming that they thought these were baboons. We were also given a tour of the townships but from the outside only as I said that it would not be safe to enter them and a white man venturing in without security would not come alive.

The townships were divided along tribal lines, the Xhosa, Zulu, Sotho, Tswana, Pedi, Coloured, Malay and Indian. The first four were far worse than the notorious slums of Kolkata and Mumbai but unlike in our country, were outside the city and shielded from the eye by fences and separated from the countryside by barb wire. The coloured and Indian townships look like any of the middle class colonies of Delhi, and Indian meant Indians, Pakistanis and Bangladeshis and all communities and religions lived happily together. There was an Indian Temple and a Mosque in the Indian Township.

We thought that our guide held extreme views, but we found out that he was only the most vocal as we confirmed his information through persistent questioning from a number of other citizens, from Xhosa, Sotho, Indian, Pakistani and coloured people we met.

We saw a street performance on the water side which called a white, a black and an Indian person from the audience to drive home the point of the rainbow coalition which was the dream of post- apartheid South Africa, but what we saw was a deep simmering resentment waiting to boil over as the change in Government did not lead to any change in the ownership pattern of assets and land and apartheid continues socially though not politically.

It may seem glib to talk of a Nation's polity after a brief visit but the little that I saw prevented me from writing another pretty travel piece on the most beautiful city in the World but it definitely made me share the ugliness that I saw creeping out between the cracks.

Chapter 24
INSHALLAH

Recently at a conference in Germany I met a fascinating English gentleman representing a Swiss company but working in the far east for the last three decades. He's comfortable with Asian culture food and languages and prefers the climate to the cold clammy weather of his homeland. He, like me, wanted to be a writer and ended up being an underwriter. He had a knack for storytelling and kept us enthralled with anecdotes so that the allotted time for our meeting was exceeded by a big margin without talking any business. Ultimately we hardly discussed business but renewed our contract with a handshake. He was well prepared with the business details and wasted no time in presentations negotiations and questions. This was the best as well as most entertaining business meeting that I attended at the conference.

Here I will share his story about his stint in Pakistan where he had opened and subsequently closed a branch of their company in the 90's. I will retell his story in first person for greater effect.

The underwriter's story -

I was stationed in Pakistan at that time because my boss wanted to be rid of me. He hoped that if I didn't resign at least a bomb, bullet or stomach bug would do me in, or I would be kidnapped for ransom which he could then refuse to pay. However, I proved to be more resilient and after a couple of years he decided to cut his losses and close down the Pakistan operations.

To help me in the process, a colleague from USA came down to Pakistan. Having heard stories and read in the newspapers about this turbulent part of the world he was quite nervous. A vigorous scrutiny on arrival at par with what people from these parts receive in the US of A did his nerves no good. He couldn't soothe his nerves with some bootleg whiskey as he was terrified of the consequences in this officially abstemious country. The fact that he had been searched thoroughly by the customs looking for liquor added to his reluctance to imbibe.

Jittery already, he boarded the PIA flight to Lahore along with me. While waiting for the flight, due to inevitable delays, he read in a newspaper that PIA was stretched for fuel and carried just enough to reach to cut costs without keeping any safety margin. This made him extremely nervous. On enquiring as to the reason for delay he was given the standard excuse, that of technical snag. This doubled his stress to near panic.

On boarding he found that his seat belt didn't work. Shakily he asked for help. The attendant responded that it's okay and we were to just hold the seat in front. We were given orange juice in cracked glasses to cheer up.

The pilot announced that the weather was bad but inshallah we should reach Lahore shortly. On my translation my friend really panicked.

Why God willing? What's God to do with it? He grumbled.

We survived the rough flight clutching the seat in front fortified by nothing stronger than orange juice in cracked glasses when the pilot announced that the ground conditions in Lahore didn't look too good but we had no choice as the fuel wasn't enough for diversion so inshallah we would land and we should hold on tight for a rough landing.

Hearing God being invoked again my friend shut his eyes and started praying audibly. But despite his prayers our plane aborted landing on the first attempt.

Now the pilot cheerfully announced that we have enough fuel for two more attempts only and not enough for diversion but inshallah he would get us on the ground one way or another.

There was complete silence from my neighbour. He was a healthy agnostic from America and didn't want to leave his fate in the hands of a heathen God especially the God of his mortal enemies.

This time however the flight landed as per the will of Allah and after a breath stopping screech finally rolled to a stop. On deplaning my colleague hastened the process of closing the branch and took an international flight on British airlines out of Pakistan and let me return to Singapore.

I need to thank Pakistan airlines and the flight to Lahore for ending my exile.

Chapter 25
CHANCE MEETINGS

This story is from the Lockdown Days. I had managed to escape the lockdown and join the LOH in Kolkata at long last.

We had been working in different cities for the last few years and I was looking forward to getting together again post retirement. But Covid played spoilsport.

The last few years of staying separately after three decades of staying together had all the flavour and fun of a clandestine relationship. This was much like our dating days when being in the same office and from different cultures we had to keep things secret till we eloped.

Of late due to frequent meetings with the ministry we could meet often but earlier we had to plan conferences and meetings with clients in the same city to get together, giving our relationship a spicy flavour.

Once going for a conference in Goa I found out her flight and seat number from her secretary and booked myself in the same flight in the adjoining seat. Then I persuaded the flight crew to let me stand with them and greet a particular passenger and show her to her seat. Hearing my story the charming flying ladies happily agreed and I gave her either a surprise or a shock by popping up with the greeting crew.

Another time I was in Hyderabad boarding a flight and she was in a hopping flight. We joked about waving at each other from the air and as chance would have it our planes were berthed next to each other. As I was on the ramp she asked me on the phone whether I was wearing an inappropriate red shirt and walking in front of the queue. Then she asked me to turn and wave as she was in the first window of the aircraft in the adjoining bay.

Given her job profile she used to visit London more frequently than I visited Lower Parel. So once, while she was there, I persuaded our Chairman to send me for a conference to London.

She's a workaholic and doing the touristy stuff together was ruled out but we had checked into hotels close by with our respective teams and planned dinner together. But she met me in the evening and said that dinner was ruled out as she had a dinner invitation she couldn't refuse and next day she had to host a dinner for her clients. I too had a dinner invitation which I was planning to bunk but now decided to accept. Comparing notes we discovered that our host was the same and so we arrived together and finally had the dinner together. The next night too I was asked to host a dinner for our clients. I happily agreed to this and I picked the same restaurant that she had recommended. So we once again ended up together with both the parties getting together. She left next day for Dubai and I too escaped to a friend's place in Surrey and had a wonderful tour of Surrey London and the nearby countryside.

During another very formal sit down dinner with place cards hosted by a European company, we were allotted different tables with strangers and waved at each other and made signs about meeting post dinner. My table mates were very impressed with the speed of my operation saying that I was able to get a date with the only Indian lady at this gathering without even speaking! They wanted to know my secret. My protests that the lady being referred to was my wife wasn't believed by anyone.

But once this plotting backfired. LOH was attending a conference in Dhaka and going there via Kolkata. I too persuaded our chairman to let me attend the meeting though it was not my subject. The kind hearted gentleman agreed and I came to Kolkata and met my daughter who was staying there those days and surprised the truant LOH at the Kolkata airport. She was surprised that I was attending the same meeting as it was not my area of expertise and was her forte.

We had a wonderful time in Dhaka and the time came for me to justify my trip by making my presentation to the Bangladeshi counterparts.

Being unfamiliar with the subject I had thought of a way out. Getting a standard presentation I had it translated to Bangla. Then I addressed the house with my sentiments at being in a country where my mother tongue was the national language and sought permission to make my presentation in Bangla. To thunderous applause I read out and displayed the same in incomprehensible Bangla ending in a standing ovation.

The next day our hosts gave us a warm Bangladeshi welcome of incredible delicacies. It was a memorable trip. But LOH was annoyed at being blindsided and upstaged by the cunning gimmick.

Chapter 26
A, MAZING EXPERIENCE

I too like many of you re read Jerome's Three Men in a Boat whenever I want to de stress. You, no doubt fondly remember the scenes where they stop over at river side pubs and your ROFL moments must be when they are lost in the Hampton Court Maze.

Recently, during a trip to England I was driving with a friend through the very picturesque Surrey country side when we stopped at an ancient pub by a canal, complete with rolling lawns, tow path, lock gates, moored skiffs, that immediately transported me back a few centuries straight into Jerome's world.

As I sat in the garden with a pint of dark English ale, I could see fellow imbibers enjoying their pints with their dogs lolling around nearby. It could be a scene from Three Men. I even had the Ploughman's lunch and a roast to live exactly like the Book.

I found out that Hampton Court was nearby and imagining that this may be the same inn where our heroes camped before visiting the Court. I immediately made plans for reliving their adventures including trying out the famous Maze.

That night, I stayed over at a charming cottage with my friend and woke next morning to a lovely sight; the lawn covered in white and a flurry of snowflakes coming down. But what looked so pretty from inside the heated cottage turned out to be a freezing nightmare outside. However, that did not deter me from venturing on to Hampton Court.

Hampton Court was everything I dreamt it would be, and the audio guide which dramatizes the experience brought alive the colourful bloody episodes of English History you may be familiar with through such books, films and TV serials like Wolfe Hall, The Other Boleyn Girl, Tudors etc. Despite the wonderful interactive display, my heart remained in the Maze. So, braving the howling winds and flurry of snow, I trudged across the lawns and gardens to the famous Maze.

It looked quite innocuous and I bravely ventured in, slightly disappointed that I won't relive the Three Men's experiences.

But, five minutes later when every twist and turn turned out to be a dead end and the buildings I could see and had kept as a landmark continued to drift further away I got a little worried. My friend too confessed that he had been in earlier in summer and on weekends when it was easy to follow the large crowds out of the Maze. But in this bleak weather when only the most eccentric would try such stunts the other visitors were scarce and as lost as we were. Soon we formed a straggly line and followed each other just as our heroes did in the book. I had a flight to catch back to India and Heathrow was close by. But now it looked as if I may miss the flight. I had visions of a slow, hungry, frozen death in the middle of some Yew hedges in Surrey. I was too embarrassed to scream help.

Finally, help arrived just as it did in the book. Some kids playing hide and seek in the Maze led us out from the entrance with much merriment. Only a half hour had passed and we laughed with relief once outside realizing the uncanny resemblance our adventure had with that of the Three Men in the Boat.

Chapter 27

TURKISH TALES

Delhi international Airport at midnight is like Sealdah station or Mumbai central or Sadar Bazaar at peak hours. Queues for immigration and security check are like going sribhumi puja or Tirupati or Lal baug cha raja Ganpati.

This is my experience of post retirement travel in economy class, without special gates to Turkey.

Indigo is a no frills airline meaning NO FRILLS. Scrunched up in cramped space shivering with cold, a baby wailing and the sound is like skewers in the brain. No blanket, pillow, eyeshade or earplugs provided. But the body is resilient especially after 1.5 hours standing in immigration and security queues. I slept and snored and between us, me and the baby kept the whole plane awake. The pilot didn't escape with a parachute because we were flying over Pakistan and Iran.

Turkey is full of cats, as Prophet loved them. Now we know why he wasn't keen on dogs.

100 years of secularism and being the heart of Christiandom is making the Islamic moves half hearted. The churches and museums are converted to mosques but the Christian frescoes are only partly covered by sheets in the inner chamber. But you can peer behind, and Jesus and the Saints reign on the outer side and passages. Even earlier Greek Roman and Egyptian images are everywhere. Dress codes and segregation are mentioned but often ignored. Dress is also largely European. Only few locals are in hijab, mostly tourists from Islamic countries. Maybe because we're staying in the European part of Turkey.

Food is amazing. Wide variety of cheese, olives, salami, sesame sweets, fruits, honey. Soup however is plain musur dal without tadka or phoron. Kebabs are dry hard and unmarinated, so not to our taste. Had the original chello Kebabs, ours is better.

This place has people from so many countries, its incredible! East Europe, Central Asia, CIS countries, North Africa, Middle East, France and no one speaks English. Except cruise ship geriatrics from USA and Indians from gulf, South Africa or England. A Bangladeshi guy sang amazing Rabindrasangeet.

Many Turks have mixed ancestors. Our guide had Greek and Bulgarian ancestors.

The Turks are extremely good looking. An average person can walk into Bollywood. And the women dress in western clothes that look like starlets giving photoshoots.

Lots of Turkish food gave Istanbul belly and I used a surprisingly clean public loo in the mosques premises, ironically, the hagia Sofia.

Capadacia is magical. The balloon ride and the underground city were unbelievable. Also did the ATV ride forgetting my age and narrowly escaped serious injury but it was an experience. Stayed in a cave hotel in refurbished ancient Greek houses.

Beaches

The extremely popular Beaches in Turkey like Kusadasi and elsewhere in Europe, including the fancy Cannes and Nice in France or the popular Brighton in England are gravelly, rocky strewn with pebbles, narrow, no surf, the water is cold, although it's very clear, clean, calm and blue, good for swimming. They're often not free, and certain rock free areas are roped off and you pay to swim.

Contrast with the Indian beaches, wide expanses of glorious fine yellow sand, roaring surf, though the water is sandy and not clear and currents often make swimming difficult and dangerous.

And even 5 star resorts aren't permitted to rope off beaches or the sea.

Despite this, hoards of sun worshippers spend so much to lie on mats on the gravel, which aren't very comfortable on all European beaches which Indians wouldn't even visit in India.

I was wondering why this is so.

Maybe our sun is too hot and grills the bathers instead of tanning them or maybe it's the fear of oglers, who are absent from European Beaches. But if the bathers are there in the multitudes, I'm sure the oglers would disappear, as it wouldn't be a rare and prohibited sight to see skin.

I also wonder why India has not become a surfing destination.

Taksem square was Street music with a Karol bag feel.

Turks have one thing in common with Bongs. An incredible and bewildering array of incredible sweets.

I fulfilled a long standing ambition as well.

I had always been envious of the government clerks who slept peacefully in public parks in the afternoons on weekdays.

Finally I did it

Sitting in a beautiful garden by the sea watching families picnicking and tourists strolling and cats frolicking, I dozed off, and spent a lovely afternoon sleeping in a park bench by the Mediterranean sea.

Kusadasi

A delicious seafood dinner on the waterfront after the sunset cruise and a vigorous swim in the incredible blue waters of the Aegean Sea, and a beer on the beach.

Pamukale

Among the hotsprings. Limestone terraces, Greek ruins, mudbath, feeling hopelessly overdressed among a sea of bikinis.

Capadacia

The incredible sunrise ride in the hot air baloon over a magical canyon.

The temptation of riding through the ravines in the spectacular Capadacia, which we had earlier seen from the hot air balloon, made me forget my age and the fact that I was never a biker dude. I was overweight and had hardly driven myself in the last dozen or so years, but still I went for the ATV ride through the canyon. It was a harrowing experience and after one accident I had to ride pillion for the last 5 kms. But at least then I could get to experience the scenes. Earlier my full concentration was on staying upright.

Chapter 28
VIGNETTES OF VIETNAM

Hanoi is just like Delhi. The hotel is like a typical one in Karol Bagh. The area is just like Karol Bagh.

The countryside looks exactly like Assam.

Indian power points work and there's jet in the loo.

Saw a 1000 year old puppet theatre in their national theatre outlining Vietnamese mythology, history, Religion and culture. It's a completely pastoral society that could be Bengal.

Wonder why USA spent so much in lives and money in their failed attempt to keep this as a colony. There's no oil or any major resource here.

Traffic is chaotic and suicidal. Crossing roads an adventure sports only Indians can attempt with panache. Europeans get nervous breakdowns. Food is exotic but vegetarians beware, everything is cooked in pork fat.

Temples of many gods and goddesses. Mother goddess is very powerful. Offering includes beer, chocolate, packed food, cookies.

Here even in restaurants you get raw ingredients and hot pot and are expected to cook it.

One of the restaurants had dog on the menu.

The unbelievable Halong bay:

Looks like the set of a Jurassic film. Actually the set of King Kong.

Went exploring caves, trekking, kayaking, boating. Tried my hand at rowing, and swimming.

After this, I can say with pride that I've swam in 3 oceans.

Groups of men sit around cooking drinking and eating on the roadside till late. It's the adda. Else it is coffee, beer and ice tea on the pavements. Both sexes. They squat on very low stools.

Teachers and exam toppers from historical times are worshipped as Gods in the temple of literature. Education was paramount after throwing off 1000 years of Chinese rule when they were 2nd class citizens.

Ghosts are part of daily life. Respected members of family.

Karma is specific. The result of each action is clearly and logically defined.

Did something hilarious while there. Through some confusion in translation, we had booked ourselves into a Vietnamese group tour to the village of Hoi An, where no one including guide or driver speaks English. It's a surreal experience.

Our official English speaking guide in Danang spoke even more spectacularly than our honorable CM. He apparently learnt it by listening to tourists. Probably mainly from Gujarat and Japan. We had an entertaining time trying to guess what he was trying to say. And of course he understood very little of anything we asked and gave random responses, mostly yes OK.

Hoi an is a most exotic place, Venice of Vietnam.

Buddha has 18 emotions in Vietnam twice as many as Indian rasas.

: A slice of medieval France in Vietnam can be seen at Bana hills French village.

The dog God and the dog pet, or dinner? There were dogs at a restaurant so I wasn't sure.

Dog is worshipped as a god and also eaten, though only in the countryside and a few niche eating places in the city

Funnily, in India we suspect that cheap eateries feed us dog and cat pretending to be mutton or chicken, but here they apparently pass off duck and chicken as the expensive dog and cat in small eateries.

Here language can be fascinating. A guide was surprised that she could understand our English. She was an English graduate. She said, "word come out of India mouth not enter my head. Maybe local language get inside word".

A very popular food is called ban cho. A Punjabi would appreciate. Others might beat up the restaurant owner.

Our driver once actually said aaaanwanwanwanwanwah in a sing song voice exactly like a petulant child throwing tantrums, and our guide understood and responded.

Vietnamese and Cambodian cuisine, are foodies delight.

Finally had frog, but they served the whole thing not just legs. Bony chewy and not too good. The French do it better.

Mekong Delta.

So far seen only in war movies especially apocalypse now.

Boat ride from motor boats to row boats to tiny dingy self rowing, village life, fantastic food, snake wine, folk music, and siesta on a hammock. Opted out of bicycle tour.

The stomach churning atrocities and the unbelievable heroic fightback by the villagers at cu chi, living physically underground for 8 years and haunting the American soldiers at night.

A very disturbing experience.

Vietnamese believe in forgive but never forget. Unlike us. We have selective amnesia.

Abhi to party shuru hui hai

The night is still a toddler.

The earlier R&R of the US army has led to a thriving scene of music, dancing and drinking in the streets and parks from evening till late at night and amazing and incredibly cheap pubs and clubs.

Of course there's objectification, but there's no stigma. Families enjoy the show together and a little girl was dancing away with the performers to the amusement of her parents.

Saigon nightlife

The famous or in? Street in Saigon, the walk Street. No traffic allowed at night. The nightlong nightlife. Music and dancing in the street. Football on giant screen. Blaring music. Cheap beer and street food.

The only difference between pavements and roads is that cars don't drive on pavements in Saigon.

Chapter 29
CAMBODIA DIARIES

Cambodia is really exotic and quaint. Very picturesque and touristy. Poor too. Food beats Vietnamese hollow. Very few people around. Airport felt like some remote railway station. Only western tourists. Asians or Indians don't come here in numbers. US dollars are the currency accepted even by street food vendors and tuk tuk drivers, the main transport. Every one seems to know English.

Off to Amkor vat, a dream of so many years.

Angkor, the lost city of 390 temples in the forest, where Indian civilization has been preserved intact for two thousand years, sanskrit is still known, forgotten Gods like Indra have temples, devotees worship Shiva, Vishnu and Budha with equal fervour, dhoti, kurta and sari are the formal wear for all occasions including marriage, vegetarianism is common, food is spicy, people are polite and there are 4 forms of namastay for different situations, and 4 kinds of smiles for every occasion. Names are Indian, food is delicious, fish is the main dish, Kulon mountain and the river of a thousand sivalingas. Swimming under the waterfall was an exhilarating experience. Everyone is friendly, even touts and hawkers aren't aggressive, rice is served with all dishes, good roads, very green countryside and architecture that makes us marvel at our ancestors.

This is now among the top 5 memorable holidays we have had Tanzania, Tuscany, Ladakh, Bangaram and Siem reip, probably 2nd most.

I was wondering why I felt so much at home in Cambodia. Then I realised that cambodeans were practically Bengalis. Here is why:

1. They have rice with every meal, preferably with sweetwater fish.

2. Restaurants have hammocks where customers can enjoy siesta after lunch.

3. Their religious food restrictions are extremely benign, anyone can keep them.

4. They're sentimental about communism despite a disastrous communst government in the past.

5. They wear dhuti punjabi to get married.

6. They've suffered major genocide, famine and civil war, but do not talk about it.

7. Even the vendors are not aggressive, despite being very poor.

8. An immense variety of street food is available everywhere.

9. They pour water over shivalingas every Monday.

10. The security guard outside the bank put up a mosquito net and went to sleep at 9 pm.

Chapter 30
TOLERANCE

Vietnam and Cambodia have some fascinating examples in toleration that can be useful examples in our increasingly polarised world.

A 1000 year Chinese rule had deeply influenced the region and Confucianism and Mahayana Buddhism were the ruling Religions, but they incorporated their earlier local Gods and Goddesses as well in their lives. Later, when Hinayana Buddhism came directly from India, the southern part embraced that. Moreover, the Gods and Goddesses of the erstwhile Hindu kingdom of Champa were incorporated, and Saraswati, Durga, Kali are omnipresent in the temples and pagodas.

When the communists took over, they did not ban Religion outrightly, but permitted it to continue as cultural heritage. Much like the neighbouring Indonesia, which though Islamic, has retained Hindu traditions as cultural heritage.

Thus, although 70% of the people declared no religion in the bio, they religiously visit temples and pagodas on the first and 15th of every lunar month and all other auspicious days, have shrines in every home, with all mobiles having both lunar and solar calendars, and offerings at the temples, pagodas, shrines are used to support the victims of USAs chemical warfare, agent orange, which is affecting even the 3rd generation since the war, and deformed children are being born.

As Hindu Buddhist and Confucian Religions tolerate other faiths and do not have any foreign allegations, they are encouraged.

However, Christians and Muslims, or their spouses aren't permitted to join army, police and government, as their origin is foreign and allegiance is suspect. Thus it is tolerance with caution.

In the neighbouring Cambodia, it is even more interesting.

An Indian king in 2nd century AD, or 2000 years ago, defeated the local tribal cave dwelling kings who called themselves Nagas, married the princess, and introduced the Brahmanical Religion here but incorporated the animist Gods native to the region, which always has been the strong point of Hinduism, and the entire nation converted to Shaivaite Hinduism.

This has an interesting resonance with the Mahabharata story of Arjun defeating a Naga king in the East and marrying his daughter ulupi and establishing a kingdom there with Brahmanical traditions. Maybe history being reflected in literature and mythology?

Later Vaishnavites took over, as in India, and Vishnu temples started replacing Shiva temples. Frequently the two factions fought till around 4th century, when a smart king introduced Harihara, half Shiva and half Vishnu. Then onwards, both deities were worshipped by all and temples had both idols, along with Ganapati, Durga, and lesser gods like Indra, Kubera and Varuna.

But Nagas continued being worshipped, and still do, as well as their mortal enemy Garuda, the vahan of Vishnu.

By then, as in India, Buddhism was in ascendancy, and a succession of Buddhist and Hindu kings, whenever they replaced each other, would change temples to pagodas and vice versa, replacing the idols inside.

But one smart king found a solution that was least problematic. When this Hindu king took over, all he did was adding a third eye to the Buddha statues, thus converting them to Shiva with minimal damage.

So when a Buddhist king replaced him, all he did was cover the third eye and Buddha was back

Around the 14th century, as the Hindus had already incorporated Buddha as an incarnation of Vishnu, the Buddhist king who built ankor vat merged the two, and the people, who were now Buddhist, worshipped Vishnu and Shiva and Ganpati and Durga alongside Buddha with equal fervour and temples and pagodas became one.

An Islamic invasion from the east around this time was defeated with Chinese help, and this ideal system of tolerance continued till the colonial rule, and survived that too, till the Maoists took over and banned all Religion, destroying images and temples with as much enthusiasm as the Taliban.

But their rule was short-lived and currently, 90 % people are Buddhists who worship Vishnu and Shiva alongside Buddha with as much devotion and ceremony.

One of the last stronghold of tolerance, which is the basic tenet of the Indian or Hindu heritage culture and Religion, thriving in this remote country while it has been struggling to survive in the land of it's origin, for almost a millenia.

Chapter 31
EATING OUT IN EUROPE

When we travel in Europe for conferences or work, we are usually taken to the better class of restaurants by our hosts, or we take out our guests at company expense, and don't bother about the price in either case. Or even when we take breaks and go around on our own, we rarely bother much about these things as we have a reasonable daily allowance in euros for the duration.

However, when travelling on our own, and spending in euros what we earn in rupees, or post retirement from our rupee retirement benefits, we learn to economise.

For example, a sit down restaurant is 2 to 3 times as expensive as a self service one, and takeaways even cheaper. Cheapest are the ready meals from supermarkets, and street food is a bit more expensive.

However it's great to go for a leisurely meal at a good restaurant occasionally to savor the experience, and try not to convert the currency in your mind. If you do, your meal would be ruined.

Second thing to remember is that water isn't free, and beer or house wines are usually cheaper. So is coke. Water comes in different brands and is either still or sparkling, but sparkling is like soda, so avoidable. I stuck to beer and wine. It's best to carry your own water, which is cheap in supermarkets, and if you buy large bottles, cheaper than beer. I still stuck to supermarket beer and wine.

Another thing, in many countries, you get money back for returning the bottles and cans, so it's smart to do so.

The best meals for the price are picnics in parks or woods or riverside or even monuments where you carry bread, cheese, cold cuts and wine. It's very popular and what the locals do most.

In France however, it's better to carry croissant, as their regular bread, baguettes, can be used as a weapon as well as food, and needs a hacksaw to cut.

It's best to find out what a dish is, as the names can be misleading. The very popular black pudding of Germany is coagulated blood, and French tartar steak is actually raw meat. A dish that sounded like cheese in Italy turned out to be cow's stomach, and in Katmandu we ordered a goats head by mistake in a Newari restaurant where no one spoke English or Hindi.

Tap water is usually free and drinkable, as is water from public fountains, and in France, most bistros give tap water for free if you ask. Du carafe I think is what you say. And in Italy the waiters are inevitably Bangladeshi, and you can order in Bangla. In France, Punjabi, Bangla Urdu or Tamil might work.

But Switzerland is another matter.

There the owners inevitably run cafés and restaurants, and except for the large chain stores, rarely employ outsiders and anyway there are hardly any immigrants in Switzerland in the tourist spots.

There, even if you ask for tap water, its chargeable, and costs more than beer in Italy.

Switzerland is horribly expensive even for those earning in dollars or euros, and their money mindedness beats all our jokes about our business communities. A meal will usually be more than 100 euros. A steak is 50 euros. Fondue 50 euros. Our neighborhood café in salt lake serves what it calls fondue at 400 rupees. After all it is molten cheese in garlic to be had with bread.

Their national dish, fondue, is quite large, and expensive. And helpings are huge, by Indian standards at least. But they do not have the concept of sharing. No 1×2 for them. And in Switzerland, if you want to, they charge you extra for sharing!

Another shocker at takeaways. We're used to picking up those little sachets of ketchup or mustard, but in Switzerland, even those are chargeable.

Swiss food like German, is an acquired taste. But Italian and French cuisines are exquisite, and worth every euro you spend on them. And incidentally, they have as little resemblance to the continental food available in India anywhere except the most posh places, as the resemblance Delhi's Bengali sweet house fare has to Bengali sweets.

Chapter 32

WASHROOMS

Being a bong, like all bongs, I have delicate belly, an obsession with food and travel combined a weakness for drinks. This resulted in experiencing various washrooms in various countries, in all kind of well known locations.

They include, amongst others, the Hagia Sophia, the world's most famous mosque, the Vatican, seat of Christianity, the Angkor vat, the world's largest temple, the Versailles Palace, homage to royalty, the metropolitan museum, temple of the sciences, and the Louvre, temple of Arts.

Thus you can see that I am truly secular in the choices of washrooms and a connoisseur of the conveniences across countries.

I had also the occasion to try out the facilities in airports in 4 continents.

The ones in the lounge are of course excellent, with showers and toiletries that you can steal, especially the traveling shaving foams. I'm still using the stock nowadays that I travel cattle class with less comfortable facilities.

I noticed with disappointment that despite all our swachata missions, public facilities outside India, even in third world countries, are much cleaner than their Indian equivalents. Although loos in trains have progressed much beyond those days when a mug used to be chained by the tap, and people rarely flushed, but still it's a far cry from the European trains.

The honor for the dirtiest airport loo goes to my hometown Kolkata, and during the periodic workers' strikes it resembles the bus station toilets in the hinterland, and takes nerves of steel and blocked nostrils to be able to use them.

This time we noticed the influence of a great many immigrants in Europe, as the trains had signs we were familiar with in India in the toilets, which we call western style toilets, please do not squat on the seats, and flush after use.

Incidentally, public toilets in Europe and North America aren't free, and the fee isn't the token one rupee or two of our sulabh sauchalayas, but a hefty 3 euros or dollars, and we poor Indian tourists converting it in rupees often lose the urge to use them.

Even in restaurants you are permitted to use the washrooms only if you've ordered something. So often we would enter a McDonalds outlet, something we never did to eat with so many exciting options available, and ordered the cheapest item usually fries and coke, in order to save the 3 euros for washrooms.

The classiest loos of course are the Japanese, but you need training and a manual to use them without mishaps, but once you've figured out the technology, it's sheer luxury, and you want to spend as much time as possible inside.

But the best facilities are available only to trekkers in India, especially in the hills. In the lap of nature, the sky above you, greenery around, scenic views and a pristine stream to wash in. Just a few things to remember, drinking water upstream from your camping area and washrooms downstream. And it's vital to remember, never camp downstream of another camp, or his washrooms become your drinking water.

Once, on a trek in the Himalayas, a lady asked our guide the way to the washrooms. The guide expansively explained, here upto the Chinese border are the ladies facilities, and here to the plains are the gentlemen's.

Chapter 33

NIPON.. A DIFFERENT SPECIE?

After a brief visit to Japan recently, what struck me the most, was incredible cleanliness, orderliness, discipline, politeness, honesty and silence everywhere.

Even in busy streets in areas equivalent of Gariahat or Karol Bagh or Churchgate, the roads are sparkling clean, there's no jostling and complete silence. Bullet train with commuters, 60 second stops and no pushing, everyone traveling in total silence.

As tourists aren't trusted to behave well, they're restricted to the last 2 compartments, but we skipped our booked seats, travelled in the unreserved compartments to get the feel.

Even in the world's busiest crossing, with the statue of the dog, Hatchiko, the one with a heart rending story, despite millions of tourists taking pictures, there was no litter. This was the case, even when there are no dustbins, due to the serial bombing involving dustbins. The locals not only carry their litter home, but also pick up after the more careless tourists.

Leave alone our cities, the great metropolitan centres of Manhattan, London, Paris, Rome, Barcelona, Istanbul are untidy bedlams in sharp contrast.

People feel upset if you count the change and are insulted if you offer tips. After the tip culture of Europe and USA and baksheesh culture back home, this was a cultural shock.

We're warned of pickpockets in Italy, France, Spain, Turkey, New York, London, Johannesburg and everywhere else, and seen plenty of examples of this, but here, they assured us that even if we leave our wallet in a park, we'll get it back untouched. I did leave cash in my hotel drawer and it was there as assured.

The petrol station attendants bow to the driver after filling the tank, and the bus driver polishes the hubcaps during stops.

Strangers are unbelievably helpful, a shop assistant left his shop to take a lost tourist to the police kiosk as he didn't speak English.

I kept wondering, are we the same specie?

But the most remarkable thing about Japan is it's public bathrooms. Absolutely free, sparkling clean and dry, and no touch required. After paying 3 Euros for loos everywhere in Europe and hoping that they're clean, and back home using them with cotton wool stuck in the nose, eyes averted and praying we don't catch unmentionable diseases, this was toilet heaven, and a typical example of the kind of people they are. More on that later.

Of course I know that they are ultra conservative, hierarchical, patriarchal, suspicious of foreigners..

Justifiable I feel … and almost robotic, but it is such a wonderful contrast to the chaotic, hostile, unhygienic noisy world outside those islands.

They do let off steam, after work, in the pubs, hanging up their coats and briefcases, they get roaring drunk and shout and laugh, but keep to themselves. No jolly camaraderie of the watering holes in the rest of the world. Even in hotel lifts, people don't meet your eye or wish you konewachi, but bow deeply if you do and respond.

I won't speak about the usual touristy stuff about Japan that you must anyway be familiar with, but touch upon the unusual things that struck me.

I will write separately about Sakura and the bomb, the octopus in the salad and the zen of art, but let me share an unknown tidbit that I came across, believe it or not!

Our own Namo is a fashion icon in Nippon ever since the international summit, with his colour combos. Earlier men's wear came in 3 colour, black, white and grey, but now 4 more are added. A lady guide admitted that women didn't watch the news earlier, but now follow him to see what he's wearing.

Moreover Indian tourists have flooded Japan, leading to warnings in loos to not stand on the seats, in one place even in Hindi.

Indian restaurants are ubiquitous, and must be avoided. Ditto Indian tourists who sing antakshari and bargain, and complain loudly frightening the locals.

The tourists apart, Japan is a wonderful experience.

Chapter 34

THE JAPANESE LOO

Marco Polo's famous book had a chapter on India that is often omitted, as researchers discovered later that he had never travelled to India but wrote the story based on stories heard from other travellers. Whatever the authenticity, I am fascinated by that account. Among many interesting things it talks about the liberated women, and warns the traveller not to be confused by their open friendliness, much as Indian travellers to the west are warned nowadays.

The aspect that deals with our story is his amazement by the fact that Indians bathed every day and still did not fall sick, and that they used only the right hand to eat and used the left for a purpose which he could not mention out of propriety.

It is this left hand job that we are talking about. This unique habit of Indians makes life difficult while travelling abroad. The paper does not appear hygienic to an Indian and leaving a wet floor is no longer acceptable in civilized society.

The French upper class discovered a wonderful substitute, the bidet. The ingenious Indian mind soon adapted it to the very useful jet which helps an Indian feel clean without creating a mess. This is now available in every home as well as most upper class hotels in India and in those foreign shores where the Indian diasporas congregates.

But hygiene and comfort in the loo has been taken to new heights by the Japanese. So much so that it can be a nightmare to a tech challenged desi like me. This is the story of my travails in this high tech ablution paradise.

I had checked into a very comfortable hotel which catered frequently to Japanese guests. The first hitch was that everything in the room was controlled by a small hand held tablet. After some help from a polite but amused young attendant, I figured things out somewhat.

But the real problems started in the bathroom. First of all, the toilet seats were motion sensitive, and the lid opened if you went near them, so that you do not have to touch anything by hand. When I approached the loo, the lid sprang open on its own, startling me. As I jumped back in surprise, it closed the lid again and flushed on its own. After convincing myself that this was not a haunted loo, and actually was more advanced technology, I managed to settle down.

The next surprise was that the seat was warm. In boarding schools in winter, juniors often have the duty of sitting on seniors seats to warm them up before these mighty seniors use the loo, and I wondered if the waiters here provided this service for the comfort of the guests. But logic suggested that such feudal service is unlikely, and this was more technology. A panel with touch screens by the side proved that this was the case. But then again, idly trying out the panel proved dangerous, as the seat became unbearably hot and caused me to jump again.

After getting the temperature under control, I was assaulted by a warm jet of water that nearly propelled me out of my seat. Further investigations proved that the panel, at the lightest touch, controlled the force direction and temperature of the jet, of which there were two, and they could even swing and rotate. The jets were followed by puffs of warm air to dry you up, and some perfume to make your stay comfortable. It was the most luxurious bathroom experience I could imagine, but a simple act of ablution took all the skill of flying a plane. Moreover, this was not a situation where you could summon a helpful waiter to give a demo and help you out.

Traumatised by the experience of the high tech luxury evacuation, I asked my colleague who hailed from the rural heartland, how he had coped. He had found a simple solution. Going back to his childhood days, when he attended to the call of nature in nature's lap, he carried the bottle of mineral water from the room fridge with him, and thus outmanoeuvred technology and luxury from coming in the way of his basic activities.

Chapter 35

SAKURA AND THE BOMB

We, along with half the world, including multitudes from India, were in Japan for the cherry blossom festival, or Sakura as they call it.

In spring, these trees sprout the pink flowers where the leaves were, after the leaves have fallen, making the trees look festooned in pink. These, over 2 weeks, fade and turn white, and then fall off, and new leaves sprout in their place.

As these trees are ubiquitous in Japan, lining most streets, crowding public parks as well as wild woodlands, gracing most public buildings and private cottages, these swathes of pink and white are no doubt a beautiful spectacle.

But cherry blossoms are available in many other countries, including India. Last year we saw plenty in Bhutan.

However, here in Japan, they're celebrated with religious fervour.

Everywhere people are out watching them, walking along them and picnicking under them.

The biggest celebration is when the blossoms fall, and people party under them.

Families do it in their backyards, where there's usually a bench under the trees.

Groups do it in public parks. Corporates send out their interns to capture spaces under trees, who stay there through fair and foul weather, braving rains and icy winds, and alert their bosses as the blossoms start falling, when everyone rushes there and then there is wine, music and dancing.

People visit the parks at night too, and the trees are lit up. This being called the night Sakura.

But why this special attachment to this ordinary phenomenon of nature?

The story goes back to one of mankind's most heinous crimes, the dropping of the nuclear bombs on innocent Japanese civilians by the USA.

The epicentre of bomb is preserved in Hiroshima as a peace memorial. They do not remonstrate or accuse, but try to remind the world of the horror so that it's never repeated again.

One of the most poignant pictures in the museum was picture of a primary school class photo, with a statement that they were all victims of the bomb. Some scorched children's clothing is also displayed. The bomb had been timed when maximum people were outdoor. Children were going to school and parents were going to work.

Generations later, people suffered from cancer, genetic diseases and birth defects as a result of the radiation.

Much the same as the American use of agent orange did to Vietnam, destroying the land and people for generations.

The Vietnamese too do not let the world forget the American atrocities, like the Jews never let the world forget the Holocaust.

We however have brushed under the carpet two bigger human tragedies, genocidal atrocities, with far greater loss of lives and uprooting of people, the 1947 partition and the 1971 massacre of 30 million people in Bangladesh.

But let us return to Japan.

The much celebrated film, Oppenheimer, a tasteless celebration of this genocide, and the American angst over it, was initially not released in Japan in order not to open wounds, but after sweeping the Oscars it was, and I read in the papers how much people were offended on the scenes of American celebration of the genocide.

But what does this have to do with Sakura?

When it was assumed that Hiroshima is destroyed for ever and nothing will ever grow there, in spring, they noticed that a few Sakura trees had survived, and a few cherry blossoms had started to bloom.

They thus became a symbol of hope, and inspiration for the Japanese resurrection.

The results are for all to see.

That is why Sakura is the national festival and its celebration is such an important factor of Japanese life.

Let me close with a hilarious news item that typifies Japanese character.

A hapless intern had laid a white sheet under a Sakura tree and was guarding it diligently for his seniors, when a group of tourists, unaware of the culture, and thinking this was for them, settled down there to party. Unable to communicate and too polite to object, while humiliated by his inability to perform his duty, the poor intern burst into tears.

Chapter 36

PONDERING IN PARIS

The first thing that strikes you about Paris is the dogs.

The city teems with them. Not strays though, like Istanbul or Thimphu, but pets on leash or baskets or even prams. Dogs of every shape and size but mostly small ones. They're almost like fashion accessories. Everyone has one or two. And they're extremely well behaved and thoroughly trained. They don't bark, fight, slobber, whine, smell butts, fawn over strangers or show any signs of life except walking occasionally.

They're everywhere. Buses, trains, metro, boat, restaurants, cafés, bars, churches, tourist spots, shops. Only place they weren't in were the galleries. Probably left in the cloak rooms with the overcoats, waiting as patiently as the umbrellas.

The second thing you notice are the brands. All clothes, shoes, watches, bags have well known brand logos prominently visible and everyone carries shopping bags with famous brand names. Exclusive showrooms are everywhere and one neighbourhood has only big brand showrooms and nothing else.

The third thing is the cafés. Italy has cafes a plenty as does most of Europe and even Istanbul, Hanoi, Saigon and nowadays Kolkata too, but nowhere are they there in such profusion as in Paris. They're lining every street.

Ah of course and the people. They're beautiful. Dressed in the latest fashion carrying off outlandish headgear, hairdo and costumes with absolute élan. They look permanently on a catwalk. Even when they're wearing very little it's still chic. And they have the bodies to carry it off. Wonder how they do it despite their excellent food and wine, which they're consuming constantly.

Public drinking is very common but it's only beer and wine and it's not only available in every grocery, mall or corner shop, but on street side shacks and with hawkers. The place is a nightmare for members of the AA.

Picknickers abound. Every bench, park, lawn, square, riverfront, steps of museums galleries and churches all have people sitting around happily eating and drinking and soaking in the sunshine.

And of course the city is dotted with galleries, museums and churches of every hue. Museums to all imaginable things and galleries for every genre of art. The churches are picturesque and offer welcome rest from tramping around or a sudden shower. Finally it's the public transport. Excellent, cheap and extremely efficient. A 2 euro ticket is valid for 1 hour in any form of transport and they're well connected and dot on time, so that travelling without a guide on your own isn't a problem at all.

But the most beautiful thing about Paris is the river Siene. It defines the city much more than the monstrosity of a cliché that has usurped the role, the Eiffel tower. The river runs right through the city, and has what looks like hundreds of picturesque bridges, each with unique architecture and sculptures, each with historic relevance or some story, like the lover's bridge or the wish fulfillment one, and many islands, and beautiful banks with people on picnics or strolling or cycling. Occasionally fishing and swimming has just been permitted after a long gap. Even the Eiffel tower with the disco lights looks pleasant reflected on the river.

Chapter 37
IMPRESSIONS OF ITALY

Italy is just like India. I didn't meet a single Italian there. Whenever I asked, 'Are you Italian?', I usually received the replies -- 'No I am Roman, Tuscan, Florentine, Neapolitan, etc.' Just like we cannot find Indians in India, but only Bengalis, Punjabis, Gujaratis, Tamilians, etc. Till 150 years ago, these were all warring city states forcefully unified by General Garibaldi. And the old animosities still remain.

Even the languages, which sound the same to us, are apparently quite different, and there is strong resistance to imposing Italian in the various districts. Vehement protests erupt if you suggest they speak dialects of Italian. They insist that they are different languages, much as Assamese were furious when their language was considered a dialect of Bengali. I noticed a street sign in Venice that was written in Italian but defaced and scrawled over in Venetian, even though the difference was only a 'Della; being changed to; De la'. Italians too, are averse to following any rules, especially in traffic.

They are vociferously argumentative about politics, government and everything else under the Sun.

Everyone alleges corruption in government and in all walks of life but seems to accept it as inevitable, much like Indians. The day-long arguments at roadside cafes and heated debates over football reminded me of Kolkata.

Graffiti too adorns every available space on public walls, though I was disappointed to note that they were of the; Romeo loves Juliet; variety rather than the witty political kind we see in Kolkata. And the habit is clearly backed by tradition; we saw graffiti, cumulated over centuries, even on the 2000- year-old ruins in Rome.

Street artists in Italy are not persecuted but encouraged and allowed to display their works alongside ancient monuments and even through street signage.

There is a great obsession with food and everyone has an opinion on which of the ubiquitous eateries are the best for which dishes. Every city specializes in a different cuisine: pizzas are a specialty of Naples where they were invented; sea food is what you should order in Venice, while steaks are the staple in Florence. For just as in India we warn people not to order bhathure in Chennai or idly in Ludhiana, there too we were strongly advised not to order a risotto in Florence.

The narrow streets reminded me of the gullys and kuchas of Banaras, Old Delhi, North Kolkata or any of the walled cities in Ahmedabad, Hyderabad, etc., except unlike their Indian counterparts they had been excellently preserved and converted into tourist attractions. We really need to learn from this.

A bit of cleaning up and some restoration and we too can create this feeling of having travelled through a time machine.

Street corners enshrine the memory of citizens killed in terrorist violence from their volatile past, and their flirtation with extreme left politics and an undercurrent of sympathy for the left and the extremists as misguided boys took me straight back to Kolkata. There too, you find numerous; Shaheed Smriti; monuments in the bylanes and an indulgence towards 'those brave boys' – the young Naxalites who gave their lives in a futile struggle for the Communist ideal.

The stoicism of the Italians is also a lot like the fatalism and jugaad, philosophy of India. Venice streets are flooded for half the year and citizens grumble and blame government apathy and greedy contractors but continue with their personal life undeterred. There are curious overturned benches in every square and street which makes convenient pathways for people to move around whenever there is flooding. Houses have shutters from the ground up to the level the water is expected to rise.

Long boots are a part of everybody's wardrobe to negotiate flooded streets. A book shop even had its display on a boat so it could float up as the water moved in. This was true jugaad Indian style.

The other thing that reminded me strongly of India was the presence of Bangladeshis everywhere.

All waiters, hawkers, street-side shop owners and sales people were Bangladeshis and one could travel through the bigger towns of Southern Italy conversing only in Bangla.

The pavements are usually blocked by makeshift shops selling shoddy products or counterfeited branded items just as you see in India, and pedestrians crowd the streets, causing vehicles to make a slow, torturous way through the crowds, their hands constantly on their horns. This again took me straight back home.

Chapter 38

IS PARIS BURNING

Is Paris burning was what a friend asked when he knew that we were vacationing in that city.

The question was answered first by our taxi driver from the airport, a Srilankan Tamil immigrant. Our driver explained that France was very liberal with documentation and though he initially came to Germany, their strict laws drove him here where he easily got citizenship. And Arab immigrants just come over the Mediterranean and settle here, getting some papers eventually.

The violence was largely restricted to immigrant localities and tourism was hit, as people cancelled plans and airlines reduced flights. So the income of people like him was affected.

The student explained that it was restricted to the Arabs who don't wish to work but take to crime for easy money and it had little to do with Religion, though religious leaders and politicians tried to make capital out of it just as they do here. Also that most perpetrators were juvenile to avoid any stringent punishment as a strategy. These things affect the lives of those who come to work hard and earn money which they cannot in their home states. Now they're all being viewed with suspicion for their skin colour and for attending the mosques.

He also hated the Bangladeshis for working below minimum wage and for longer hours thus ruining the market. This boy's car was burned too, but he was confident of getting compensation through insurance. A contrast to how public views our insurance companies.

The Bangladeshi waiters I met were Buddhist, fleeing persecution from fundamentalists at home, and being viewed as being a part of their tormentors here because of skin colour. However their employer, a French lady, was extremely complimentary about them and had promoted one of them as the chef when the French chef retired in an iconic French restaurant near Louvre. She said that they run the place for her now as her father is too old, and kept the ancient family business alive.

The final image is from the most vibrant part of Paris, the artists quarters at Montemarte. The lawns and steps of the cathedral were jam packed with picnicking groups, live music, drinking and dancing by locals, immigrants, tourists, everyone. This included a group of Arab teenagers playing Arabic pop and drinking and jiving right on the doorstep.

This had me wondering. Back home in their country or even in India, they would have been murdered by their imams for the sacrilege of drinking and playing music, leave alone doing so outside a mosque and by the temple or church management for the sacrilege of doing so on their doorstep. Here, no one batted an eyelid.

This, I think, is civilization. Racism, bigotry, intolerance, fundamentalism, politicians and religious leaders cannot take it away.

In islands like this, Paris isn't burning.

Chapter 39
STORIES OF SPAIN

Spain is the 7th European country that we've spent at least a week in. Though a bit like France outwardly, it was quite distinct, as we discovered in about two weeks spent going around the country, but mostly in the South.

The people I thought were friendlier, and very good looking. Bit like the Italians. The country is poor. There are more beggars, petty thieves, homeless people scavenging garbage bins than I've seen elsewhere in Europe.

People are laid back. Siesta is all important. Everything closes between noon and five in the evening and nothing is open on Sundays. Reminds me of Kolkata, Goa, and Cambodia. Pubs and Cafes do brisk business and are omnipresent. People spend hours sitting and talking over Beer or Sangria. Bit like Italy. Like Italians, they're proud of their separate regional identities and have different languages, food and culture, though to us it seemed very similar. They've had a violent history, both in medieval times, then the inquisition and finally the extremely tragic Civil War. Politics continues to be highly polarised and strong separatist movements exist.

People are vocal about opinions. Despite 800 years of Islamic rule, not much remains except for the strong influence in the art, architecture and cuisine in the south. Every mosque was destroyed and churches built on the ruins. The famous Cathedral in Cordoba was spared but altered and turned into a Cathedral. The Muslims were given option of converting, leaving or getting killed. Thus there is no indigenous Muslim population. Later, both Jews and Protestants met with the same fate and the country is vehemently Catholic.

South Spain is straight out of tourist brochures. Dazzling blue skies, sparkling blue sea, palm trees, brilliantly whitewashed houses, castles nestled on hilltops, in fact a lot like the French Riviera or the Adriatic coast of Italy with a slight oriental air, and one fantastic improvement... unlike the rest of Europe, the beaches are not pebble and gravel but actually of sand. I often wondered how people sunbathed on such prickly surfaces. Here there was no such problem and the sand was dotted by prone sun worshippers, mostly topless.

Their national dish and obsession is paella, a rice dish that's a cross between biriyani and khichri, and has meat in the north and seafood in the south. But the ubiquitous snack is tapas, which could be anything from potatoes, bread, seafood, meat, vegetables, pickles or croquettes in small bite sized portions. One piece is offered with any drink you order, even water, at any cafe or bar, which dot every street and plaza. They are also very proud of their ham, and it's displayed everywhere, with popular restaurants being called museum of ham. Beer and Sangria are the popular drinks but there are regional variations. Every city has its traditional food and drink or variations of regular drinks. Like Madrigo of Madrid, from a berry, just like Amarula of South Africa. The sparkling wine of Spain is Cava and some cities only serve Cava cocktails instead of the ubiquitous Sangria. The national dessert is Churro and chocolate and there's an iconic outlet where everyone from Antonio Banderas to Penelope Cruze and Princess Diana to Pete Sampras have visited, and their photos adorn the wall. Its open from 5 am to 1 am, and there are queues to enter. It actually was quite wonderful and better than the churros we ate everywhere else.

Most low end jobs are done by immigrants from the erstwhile colonies, like everywhere else in Europe, but here they're entirely from South and Central America, as they have the language in common. Therefore beautiful Latinas dot the markets and distinctly native American features are common. Their national sport is the very controversial bullfighting, and it has been banned in some states, but elsewhere it's still a major obsession and matadors are national heroes. At Saville, they take the art very seriously and appreciate nuances. Elsewhere it's a boisterous blood sport that shocks current sensibilities, but you cannot deny the adrenaline rush.

Finally the Gypsy flamenco is a spectacle quite unlike any other dance forms I've seen. Perhaps tap dancing evolved from it. Said to be descendants of the banjaras of India, they have distinct features and are a big part of the tourist experience. We thoroughly enjoyed our 2 weeks in the Iberian Peninsula but opted out of visiting Portugal which has a very similar culture.

Spain is justly proud of its food, music, art, architecture and culture and their seafaring history. If Columbus had a better sense of Geography, we might have been speaking Spanish today, Spain would have been far richer and probably have an Indian origin President by now.

Chapter 40

MY BRIEF CAREER AS A MATADOR

The controversial national sports of Spain is bullfighting. The woke brigade get apoplectic at the mention. The testosterone charged get orgasmic at the sight of blood and gore.

Some states have banned the sport and in some it's ignored, but in Seville it has the status of high art and it's the blockbuster sport of Madrid.

The top matadors earn 1 million euros per fight or up to 3 million a day. And they become national heroes. After the fight they're carried out on shoulders of the fans, but occasionally on stretchers also, as sometimes the bull wins.

Careers of matadors aren't long, and most iconic matadors have died in the ring, or retired after a crippling injury, as we discovered in the hall of fame at Madrid's bullring. There was only one legendary female matador on the wall of heroes, so I guess that's one more glass ceiling broken in this most macho of sports.

The season was over when we reached, so there was no real fighting to witness, and I wasn't sure whether it was a good thing or not.

After visiting the ring, the museum, seeing the films etc., there was one experience that we could have, that is experiencing the adrenaline rush of the matador vicariously, through AI.

We put on a cape and wore the mask which transported us to the ring. With roaring crowd and the snorting bull, we have to make the moves and dodge the bull, making as close passes as we dare. Just like the real matadors, except that you can neither be killed nor get hurt.

I was initially hesitant, but when a petite and jolly Moroccan fellow tourist in a hijab took the plunge and pranced around with great swagger, I too decided to brave it.

As usual, my uncanny sense of directions took over and I couldn't find the bull. But when the roar of the virtual audience warned me, I noticed that the bull was behind me.

After a narrow escape, and some more clumsy passes, I was beginning to get the hang of it and started to enjoy myself. The incredible adrenaline rush, made me try the daring close passes, reminding myself that the bull isn't real.

Incidentally that day was the world cup semifinal, as I was rooting for Kohli's record breaking century.

There was one more fellow Indian in our group, and he was following the match and updating me.

And just as the bull was rushing, he shouted, century, which I heard over the roar of the virtual spectators, and turned around to cheer.

The next thing I knew was the bull getting me squarely on the back and sending me flying. Though there was no pain, the fright was real.

Thus ended my all too brief career as a matador.

Chapter 41
DRUK DIARIES

Bhutan, or raised land in Sanskrit, bhu uthan, is called Druk, or dragon by the natives.

It's a country being formed, the youngest Buddhist nation, since the 8th century, when guru Rinpoche, or Padmasambhava who went there from India via Tibet, and introduced the Vajrayana philosophy which is the state religion. It happily incorporated all the existing animist deities who still thrive in the monasteries, and in nature.

From being a no man's land of nomadic herders, it unified under another monk in the 16th century and became a nation just a few centuries ago under the Wangchuck dynasty, whose extremely enlightened 5th ruler reigns today.

Even the mythology happens just a few hundred years ago and not in some prehistoric time, and everyone seriously believes in, especially reincarnation.

Democracy is just decades old, and the king volunteered to share power, give himself a retirement date and give power to his parliament to remove him. He leads a very simple life in a modest home like any other citizen and his children walk to the neighbourhood government school.

To enter politics one needs to be a graduate with 5 years of government service.

TV, internet and mobile phones have been introduced recently but to maintain the culture, everyone speaks the same language, Dzongkha, and wears the same dress, Go and Kira.

All houses have the same design and colour scheme and all plots are of the same size.

Everyone knows English, which is the second language.

Cigarette is banned, as is plastic, and killing of any living creature.

Hunting, mountain climbing and skiing are prohibited so as to not disturb the spirits that live on the mountains. Most people are vegetarian, and all meat products imported.

Food is largely rice chilli and cheese and various veggies in different combos, called datshi, emma datsi being ubiquitous, for all 3 meals. Ara is the popular drink, very much like sake.

Local whiskey is also very popular.

There are 20 districts in 5 regions, and visitors basically see the relatively accessible and populated western parts, mainly Thimphu, Paro and Punakha. We also visited Pubjiko, where the black necked cranes winter and has a fairy tale monastery.

Entry is through Phutshiling on the border. The moment you enter the contrast is striking.

From the congested chaotic noisy dirty border town in India you enter a quiet neat sparkling clean and spacious town.

You climb up through pristine scenery and various checkpoints with polite army ladies confirming your visa and permit till you reach any of the picturesque towns with beautiful spacious resorts and breath-taking views.

The people are extremely polite and friendly and language is never a problem.

You visit the monasteries and forts, local markets and villages, including the showcasing of erotica, the village and monastery of the divine madman, a very colourful 14th century Saint, whose legends would not be allowed on social media.

If you find Bhutanese cuisine too hot there's Indian and continental food everywhere.

The culmination is the climb to the Tiger's nest, a monastery perched almost impossibly on a cliff a daunting climb of 1.2 Kms vertically upwards, 14 Kms in all which you have to complete as staying up there isn't possible. But it's worth every bit of the pain, and a traditional hot stone sauna will revive you.

You return satiated, that you have witnessed shangri-la hidden quietly, even now in the 21st century.

Chapter 42
TIGER'S NEST

This story is about me, striking one more item off my bucket list. We climbed the tiger's nest.

Finally after many missed opportunities we were travelling in Bhutan and on the penultimate day had planned to do this.

It was raining the night before, and the morning was cloudy, with the monastery covered in fog when we started the climb.

My wife had read up extensively on this and was totally pessimistic about making it.

The beautiful climb through pine trees with spectacular views made us plan to take photos and enjoy the ambience on the leisurely climb down while we huffed up the steep slopes.

A majority of the people returned from the cafeteria at the halfway point. By now the sun was out and the majestic sight of the fairy tale castle high up on a cliff was visible.

By the time we reached the second view point most climbers turned back. Because here when you think you've made it, there's 700 steps going down and another 250 up. Our guide assured us that we can make it, and although exhausted, we did. Inside there were another 60 odd steps, steep, reminding us of Ankor Vat, but as an American exclaimed, the pain was worth it.

Cameras aren't allowed in, and the atmosphere is mystical and overpowering, while you meditate in the cave, listen to the mythology, and view the iconography.

Exhilarated, we started to return.

While climbing we had decided to turn back when we were tired, saying faiz ki rah sarbasar manzil, jahan bhi pohonche kamiyab aye.

But as one cannot stay up there, we had no option but to return immediately.

Climbing back those 700 steps up we thought would be the toughest job, but that was over before we realized it.

Now we were congratulating ourselves as being one of the very few senior citizens among the Indians who managed this.

By now my wife being 2 years younger, 20 kgs lighter and having led a disciplined life of moderation and yoga, started galloping like a gazelle and disappeared from view.

I, having led a life of excesses and sloth, started rueing my massive beer belly and 20 kgs excess fat.

Till the midpoint I managed to keep up, but after lunch my body started protesting vehemently. By now it had started to drizzle and we hurried down to avoid a downpour.

All ideas about appreciation of nature and preserving memories through photographs were dropped in trying to hurry down.

It started to snow but the beauty was masked in the pain, and I was sweating profusely in the sub zero temperature, till my clothes were drenched and I thought icicles might form on my forehead.

Finally my legs declared a strike.

Here our driver became my guardian angel and leant his shoulder to my 90kg plus load, helping me limp on. A very effusive American lady kept cheering me on and stayed along till we reached the parking lot.

Our guide was waiting there anxiously and relieved to find me staggering back took me quickly to the car where the LOH was calmly relaxing.

It took us 7 hours, excluding time for lunch, tea and visiting the temple.

The next stop was a hot stone bath, the traditional Bhutanese sauna to revive us and relieve the pain, followed by a strong drink, a hearty dinner and a good sleep.

This was one of the most memorable parts of our magical trip to shangri-la.

Chapter 43
CALCUTTA CAMEO

During a recent visit to my hometown – the city that defies definition, a couple of scenes, framed by the rattling windows of the city's cacophonic local buses, stay frozen in my mind.

The first was outside a graffiti-covered public conveniences opposite a medical college, where the integrated easing of Hindus, Muslims, Sikhs and Isahis, aided by a mild shower, inundated the cratered sidewalks. A series of strategically placed half bricks formed a bridge across this stream. A bevy of pretty young leftist student activists, saris delicately lifted with one hand, placards clutched in the other doubling as umbrellas, protecting their heads from the drizzle, balanced precariously while crossing this bridge all the while loudly heralding the death of American imperialism in sweet falsetto. On the way, the revolutionaries passed a nameless wayside shrine. In flagrant contempt of the indoctrinated instructions, the arms raised in slogan were brought down in genuflection, paying obeisance to the opium of the masses. The traffic jam eased. My bus moved on.

The second was the mouth of a micro narrow lane called, say, Baker Street, leading off a busy thoroughfare. This lane was famed for its many gourmet ethnic eateries. The street was evenly paved with slime. A few feet from the entrance, on a ledge on a wall, a kebab joint did roaring business. A plastic sheet held up by a contraption of ropes, poles and bricks, protected the customer's eye – but presumably not his nose – from a huge pile of festering garbage a few feet away. Numerous people stood in the slight drizzle devouring prawn cutlets and tangri kebabs on the lee side of this sheet. Right opposite a dimly lit signboard on top of a dull red doorway proclaimed: "Valentino's Bar (airconditioned)". A two-foot square space outside the door was paved with red tiles and was free from slime. A uniformed doorman stood passively by on one side. The graffiti covered walls on the sides were adorned by many posters, some torn and fluttering. Prominent among them were two identical large posters, fairly new, advertising some sports magazine which displayed large attractive blow-ups of Steffi Graf. A nude lunatic, one of the city's many such strays, was staring entranced at these. He next gave each poster in turn a smacking kiss and seemed entirely pleased with himself. My bus moved on, shifting the scene from my window.

This was not a cliché from a pseudo-surrealistic film at Nandan (or Sakuntalam, as the case may be) but a frozen scene from the drama of Calcutta. This, it seemed to me, was the essence of the city we hate to love.

Chapter 44

TRAVELLING IN THE RAIN

The deluge that is drowning Mumbai, but failing to dampen its spirits, sent me back down the memory lane.

It feels wonderful to sit on the balcony and watch the rains lashing the trees, with accompanying sound effects of the whistling wind, getting pleasantly drenched in the spray, a forced holiday as the roads are impassable, and a cheering mug in hand. High spirited Mumbaikars are making most of the unforeseen holiday by gathering at Marine Drive and other spots by the sea, ignoring danger warnings, to get drenched in the waves. The mind's eye started a series of flashbacks, of the pleasures and pains of being caught in the rain, away from the cosy shelter of home.

The first two stories are retold in detail elsewhere, so the impatient reader can skip to the third.

It was in the 80s, my wife and I were backpacking across South India. Having lived in the North, and having travelled and trekked in the Himalayas, we discounted the idea of cold in the Southern climes, and carried no warm clothing in order to travel light. Thus we went up

186

to Kodaikanal in light Tshirts and shorts, our usual travel wear.

We had heard of a Tibetian dhaba for good economical food and congenial atmosphere, and walked down there for dinner. It was raining, and unexpectedly chilly, and the shack was warm, the owner friendly, and food delicious. After a week of vegetarian south Indian food, the momos, thukpa and chang was heaven-sent, and we blessed our informant. These were the days before the net, social media and smart phones, word of mouth being the only source of information.

The rain soon turned into a downpour, and the locals predicted that it would go on all night. To add to the fun, the lights went off. The concerned owner called our hotel, but was informed that no taxis were available. Efforts by the helpful locals and the owner also failed to unearth any conveyance, the town being an early sleeper, and the rains and power cut had forced all taxi operators indoors. Walking to the hotel in pitch dark and pouring rain was not possible, even with the loans of umbrellas, torches and directions offered. Apologetically, the locals left for their homes. The owner wanted to shut shop, but couldn't turn us out, so offered us some shawls to ward off the chill, and more hot soup and chang. The only other occupant was an ageing European, evidently one of the regulars, who had had quite a few and was sleeping it off. We were told that he had wandered into town and never left, having settled down in a cottage in the forest. Anyway, he woke up, mumbled something and left. The owner, apologetically offered us the benches and some newspapers to spend the night, and proceeded to lock up. We were shivering and cursing our luck, when a loud honking startled us. Peering out, we saw a lifeline in the shape of a massive battered old imported car, headlights blazing, and our previously somnolent co guest at the wheels, beckoning to us. The beaming host explained that having seen our predicament, he had woken up some unfortunate taxi owner, borrowed his wheels, and was offering us a lift to our hotel.

We gratefully jumped in, and after what seemed an interminable ride through the pitch dark night, howling winds and thundering rain, we reached our hotel, and his insistent honking got them to open the gates and let us in. He merely nodded to our profuse thanks. Throughout, we had hardly exchanged any words with our Good Samaritan saviour.

The next flashback is of Chail. We were staying in the palace, or rather, in some huts on the premises, in this Palace in the middle of the forest, atop a hill overlooking Shimla in Himachal, built by the Maharaja as a love nest for his English paramour, who eloped with him from the British summer capital. It was the nineties, and we had a child. We were enjoying a lazy vacation in this isolated peaceful retreat, high in the Himalayas.

One day, we planned a short one day trek, to the neighbouring hilltop, eight kilometres away, to visit the shrine of an ancient tribal Goddess favoured by the local herdsmen. We left the car in the Palace, and little one in tow, packed lunch in backpack, we walked through the pristine forests. Enjoying the pleasant sunshine on the hilltop meadow, I was trying to catch a nap, when a cold water droplet rudely woke me up. We noticed that ominous black clouds were boiling in, and being heralded by menacing thunder rolls and lighting flashes. The Goddesses tiny shack providing little shelter, we decided to hurry back, trusting the shelter of the pine forest. Kiddo on my shoulder, we started off at a brisk trot. Luckily, or so we thought, it was downhill all the way. Within a quarter hour, the deluge caught up with us, and we cursed our idiocy in not driving up at least till the dirt track. The path became muddy and slippery, and we were soaked to the bones, shivering in the cold, stumbling down in zero visibility. The frequent lightning kept us from seeking shelter under the pines. After what seemed like ages, a hut loomed out of the mist. We had reached the tiny hamlet. We huddled into its solitary teashop, where some villagers were seeking shelter, and were immediately welcomed in by the concerned locals. We were given blankets, placed by the fireside, and plied with hot tea. We were also offered dry clothes, and soon our baby was swaddled in colourful Himachali attire. A boy was despatched to the Palace to get a car, and eventually, we returned to our snug cottage, expressing heartfelt gratitude to our saviours.

The third memory is of the Terai, in North Bengal, bordering Bhutan, at the forest rest house of Jhalong. The rest house was a wooden cottage on stilts, to keep away wild animals and floodwater, and situated right by a waterfall, whose roar drowned everything and made conversation difficult. The chowkidar cooked our evening meal and left for the village before dusk, leaving us alone in the forest with no means of communication. The dim lighting was provided by solar lamps. Our kids, two by now, were demanding ghost stories to go with the atmosphere. When suddenly, an uproar started, drowning out the roar of the waterfall. It was as if a bucket had been overturned on top of us, and it crashed on our tin roof. Simultaneously, the wind started screeching and wailing. Branches were falling with crashing sounds, and as if on cue, the light conked out. The whole cottage rattled, and it felt as if the roof is about to blow off. In the pitch dark, sudden lightning flashes were the only light, blue, bright and frightening. The roof steadily leaked in a dozen places. My rum induced bravado vanished. A better setting for a ghost story couldn't be created, but no one was in a mood for it now. We sat huddled together, and at some point, dozed off.

Next morning dawned bright and crisp, with sunlight glinting off snow peaks, and the forest looking green and washed, the sky a sparkling blue. The forest guard was back, bringing tea and pakoras for breakfast. It was just another monsoon night in those foothills. These are wonderful memories now, but I think that nowadays I would rather enjoy the rains snug from my balcony.

Chapter 45

THE HONEY TIGERS

Recently during the puja break I had visited my hometown Kolkata after more than a decade. After the initial nostalgia was crushed by the unimaginable crowd of enthusiasts I desperately wanted a break.

As an antidote I decided to visit two absolutely deserted destinations within a few hours distance from Kolkata, mandarmoni and the sundarbans.

Mandarmoni, thanks to the environment activists was totally deserted with pristine beaches.

Sundarbans however has changed for the worse. Resorts have sprouted all over the villages and tourists come for a picnic playing loud music and insisting on elaborate meals.

My earlier visits had been rather luxurious where you stay aboard a steamer and it's a gastronomic tour with Bengali delicacies and comfortable cabins. This time my daughter had booked a backpackers tour with home stay in a village and a small boat to explore the creeks and even a jungle walk, something unheard of in the area.

The village was like a painting of rural Bengal, breathtakingly pretty.

191

Electricity had arrived a couple of years ago but was still erratic. It is approachable only by boat. This was the last village before the forest and our guide boatman and accompanying forest guard were all local.

It was a serene vacation floating around the immense delta among the mangroves all day and back to the village in the evening. Excellent food of locally caught fish of varieties I had not heard of. The walk was extremely difficult in the knee deep mud. Wildlife sighting was rare and that was as expected for the area.

Next morning there was a disturbing news of one of the villagers out crab fishing in a creek towards the town rather than the forest was killed by a tiger. Although his comrades had driven the tiger away and rescued him, he died before they could reach the nearest road head. Apparently this is part of life for the people of these islands.

The forest guard narrating the incident gave us many insights into the closely linked lives of the villagers and the infamous man eaters of sundarbans. Some facts are known through books and films but some were quite extraordinary.

He said that the researchers know only the superficial stories of these impenetrable mangroves but the real tales are told by the honey gatherers who penetrate deep inside.

We know that tigers can swim for miles and attack only from the rear and often take men off the boats. They can also leap twenty feet and boats in the creeks are easy prey. The lack of natural prey due to increased salinity and rising water levels has forced them into hunting the men.

As fishing and honey gathering are the only livelihoods available, confrontations are inevitable. Ironically for an area which is mostly water, sweet water fit for drinking is scarce and animals and humans tend to congregate in the few sources of rainwater fed ponds that dot the human settlements.

The government tried to introduce masks to be worn on the back of the heads to fool the tigers but within a year they saw through it. Strategically placed nets masquerading as traps are now used to keep the tigers from entering the villages but the lure of the livestock and stray dogs and occasionally people tempts the tigers into encroaching on the home ground of their encroachers.

But the most unique story came from the honey gatherers. These brave souls search the forest from the boats and follow the bees to find the hive. Then leaving a boatman to guard, they land in the mangrove forest and reach the hive to smoke out the bees and collect the honey. Apparently the tigers have figured this out and wait by hives as a hunter waits by a bait. Sometimes they prey on the distracted gatherer at the edge of the group and sometimes the lone boatman, always attacking from the right rear to incapacitate the arm that holds the axe or weapon.

Even more intriguing is that they have started eating the honey themselves. The technique is that the tiger rolls in the mud and lets it dry to create a mud shield against stings. Then they leap into the air to knock down part of the hive. As most of the bees swarm back to the remaining part of the hive, the tiger rushes to the river with the broken hive and puts it in the water. This drives out the remaining bees and the tigers enjoy a rare dessert in this saline marshland. We were awestruck by the story of the ingenuity of the king of the jungle worshipped here by both Hindus and muslims as dakshin rai. In the current atmosphere of mutual suspicion even these remote areas are sadly infected and the imams forbid their flock from worshipping idols while the Hindus have started calling the Muslim deity ban biwi as ban devi thus endangering another unique culture of a Muslim goddess and a hindu God being worshipped in a temple together by both communities.

Chapter 46
VIEW FROM THE LOO

There is a joke about the man who went to the loo without his phone and found out the number of tiles in the bathroom.

I do not have this problem as I read in the loo and I have a library of thrillers, best sellers and magazines to keep me occupied during the time in this very private space.

However the view from the loo is usually bathroom tiles and fittings and possibly toiletries and towels.

But there are a few notable exceptions and I will share some of them.

We were staying in a fancy resort which tried to give us the feeling of being one with nature. The loo, accordingly had a small enclosed garden next to the window to give an impression of being in the middle of nature whilst in the loo. It was a slightly uncanny feeling of doing your business in the open as we had to while on treks in the remoter parts of the country.

The other spectacular view was from a lodge in Sikkim which was situated on the edge of a Ridge and we had a panoramic view of snow peaks from all the rooms, the balcony and also from the loo. This was safe as only someone with the ability to fly, could actually look inside. One could spend this long time in reflecting whilst viewing the beautiful Himalayas whilst sitting on the throne.

But the most extraordinary view is from the forest lodge in Holong in the Jaldapara tiger reserve. This particular lodge is in the middle of the forest, next to a small stream and overlooking a salt lick. This was earlier reserved only for an iconic chief minister of the state but has since been open to the public and if you were lucky enough and book months in advance you may get this particular room.

Not only from the balcony but from every room and every window we could see various animals coming to the Salt lick and to the stream as if they are there for our private viewing.

This marvelous view was available even from the loo and I had the unique experience of having my morning contemplation in solitude on the throne interrupted by a battle Royale going on outside between a rhino and his challenger.

In the early morning mist the grunts and thumps got my attention and I was witness to a scene which lucky photographers get to see after months of patient stalking. And here I was getting a ringside view of this spectacle while sitting in the loo.

This definitely would be the ultimate view from the loo.

Chapter 47
EGG IN A CAVE

I had always wondered at the brilliance of the man who first invented omelettes. To look at the dirty round shells emerging from the rear end of birds, which contain a smelly yellow liquid when broken, and to dream up these fluffy golden delicacies took a man of imagination and enterprise. Or a woman, I don't want to be shunned by my family.

So I flew back a hundred millennia, landed in a lush tropical forest and zoomed down on a scene unfolding below.

A Stone Age man, wearing less than Salman Khan, was cautiously creeping down a clearing, clutching something close to his chest. It was a bunch of huge eggs, of an ostrich perhaps, or some now extinct species like the Dodo. He was keeping a wary eye out for predators, I felt. I followed him. We came across the remnants of a bush fire, burning embers, blackened tree stumps, smoke rising everywhere. My fly senses soon detected a stench. I noticed that my caveman had smelt it too, and followed his nose much like I did. I decided to call him Ungh, from the sound he seemed to be making when excited. We came across a brutal scene.

A wild boar, to escape the fire perhaps, had taken refuge in a mud hole, and had been charred to death there. Excited, Ungh hurried to the spot, looking for a feast. In his hurry, he stepped on a flat rock that was still red hot and went flying, scattering eggs everywhere. The eggs crashed on the rocks, spilling their contents. Ungh looked dismayed. He had no means of carrying the spilt insides back to the cave. But he noticed that something funny was happening. The liquid yolk that had spilled on the hot rocks, instead of running into the mud, were spluttering and turning golden and solid. Forgetting his pain, Ungh stuck his finger in the stuff, and tasted it. His face showed delight. He proceeded to tear bits of the fried boar and bits of the fried eggs and had a hearty feast. I realized that I was witnessing the birth of the quintessential British breakfast of Bacon and Eggs, and also that English cooking hasn't evolved in a hundred thousand years.

But this still wasn't the omelette, so I decided to follow him home. There was Mrs Cavewoman, wearing less than Sunny Leone, so I will call her Ufff.. I noticed a raw wound on her head, so realized that they were newlyweds. Ungh tried to describe the new delicacy with excitement, and offered her some. She wasn't impressed, and when he couldn't explain how it was made, made disparaging grunts. Some things, I realized, haven't changed in a hundred thousand years.

Uff went back to survey the source of this new food. Her quick intelligence figured out the secret, and she carried back some smouldering sticks. Soon, a blazing fire adorned the cave much to everyone's amazement. And on some rocks heated on this fire I saw Uff adding various bits of green stuff she had gathered, some rock salt, and crack more eggs to pour out the stuff within, throwing bits of game in it too. A wonderful stuffed omelette emerged, the first in the world. Uff must have been French.

More myths busted, the world's first scientist and chef were women!

I decided to return with my findings to the kind Admins. Later I will try to find who invented the Chole Bature. And if my readers are convinced that this story wasn't herbally inspired, I will reveal the secrets of Jerusalem and Kurukshetra.

Chapter 48
GHANTI

There is a mythical land in Indian legends where beautiful celestial creatures who are exquisite musicians and dancers called Kinnaurs and Kinnauris live, somewhere in the Himalayas, near the abode of the Gods.

These legends were no doubt born from travellers' tales from explorers of the remote Himalayan region adjacent to the Tibetan plateau, currently called Kinnaur, a district in Himachal Pradesh.

Having come across many references to this unearthly place in our classical literature, when we heard of a trekking expedition to this area asking for volunteers, me and my wife immediately applied, and went through the required interview, medical tests and police verification required, as this was then a part of the inner line, on the disputed border with China, and tourists were not allowed in. There were no roads, and it was almost inaccessible in the eighties, which added to the charm.

On the lone daily bus that went to Sarahan, our base camp, we met our fellow team mates, the majority of whom we found out to be fellow Bengalis from their unique Hindi accents. My wife was immediately inducted as a honorary Bengali and the default mode of communication became Bengali, as it inevitably happens wherever bongs congregate.

The real trek started from Karcham, and we were in the wild, scarcely populated mountains, climbing up goat trails and camping by the mountain streams.

In our first camp we understood what gave birth to the legends of these astral beings. A group of villagers, hearing rumours of strangers in their midst, came exploring, bearing food drinks flute and drums and despite the language barrier treated us like honoured guests or long lost friends. Bonfires were set up, music started, and we were all pulled into a conga line of slowly weaving folk dances, sensuous and magical in the firelight, under the Photo by twinkling stars, the distant roar of the river and the dark looming mountains ahead. It was definitely a dreamlike scene. The men were handsome, the women bewitchingly pretty, the clothes colourful, the music haunting, the atmosphere intoxicating, all the more for having imbibed in liberal quantities the nectar of the gods; the apple, apricot and grape liquor called Ghanti.

They left with lighted torches later in the evening, leaving us ample stocks of apples, apricots, bits of dried game meat and ghanti. Next day we trekked on with the ghanti replacing the water in our backpacks.

This scene was repeated at every camp till we crossed the tree line, and even then some villagers climbed up with us just for the company, singing, playing their instruments and plying us with goodies. One incident was a little unpleasant but funny. Misinterpreting the friendliness of the ladies as an invitation, a few boorish men decided to visit a village at night, as the pretty ladies had extended the invitation to us all to drop in for ghanti or a meal anytime. Many of the men worked in the cities or on road works, and the ladies managed the farms orchards and livestock. But as they tried to act fresh, they were promptly thrown out and chased back to camp by the ferocious Tibetan mastiffs that guarded the villages.

Having crossed the Kinnaur Kailash pass without mishap, we came down to pleasanter climes and our last camp was at Kalpa, from where the road was a short walk away and a bus would be available next day to take us back to Sarahan and onwards to Shimla. We were in a relaxed mood. It was to be a full moon night. We were visited by a delegation from a nearby village with a different sort of invitation. The village had a fair on the full moon with all night celebrations of music dancing food and drink and we were to be the honoured guests. All the villages in the area would attend.

We were really excited at the prospect of seeing this rarely witnessed festival which is the stuff of myths and legends. Accordingly we were escorted to the village where a huge welcome awaited us. One lady had a delicacy in her home which was very scarce in those areas; tea. The ladies in our group made a beeline for that home. The menfolk drowned us in Ghanti and they themselves, irrespective of age or gender were pickled in it, giving the music and dance additional vivacity.

This was truly something from mythology; moonlit night, snow peaks glittering on the horizon, eerie music, enchanted beings swaying to the music and drawing us into their rhythms.

The food on offer was less ethereal, goat entrails, local sausages called gimpi, and other exotic fare.

As dawn approached, none of us were in a position to walk back to camp down those mountain trails. So we were practically carried down in procession by the singing Kinnars and Kinnaris, holding lighted torches and playing their instruments, but the songs they were singing were not their haunting folk melodies, but bawdy Bengali songs that we had taught the whole village that night.

So if an intrepid traveller today finds that the green hills of Kinnaur come alive not to the sound of celestial music of our folklore, but bawdy Bengali ballads sung to the folk tunes of a distant humid land, do not think that the heavens have been overrun by the denizens of Patalpuri, but blame it on Ghanti.

Chapter 49
CHANG

During our University days, the cheapest tipple that gave a kick for the buck and was relatively safe, was a whitish smelly concoction called Chang, brewed by the Tibetan refugees living in a shanty town by the Yamuna, in an area ironically named Majnu ka tila.

At the affordable price of two rupees for a plastic jug full, which held eight helpings, it was enough to keep two young men in high spirits. It was served in a dirty shack, peopled by labourers, rickshaw pullers, hawkers, petty criminals, and students; the general underbelly of society.

This was actually rice beer, which is mildly alcoholic, and is the staple household drink in Nepal and most of our hill states, and an essential part of hill life, taken by all, and even used as offerings at monasteries. But the brew served at the Tibetan dhabas, or Tibdhabs as we called it, was more potent stuff, adulterated with cheap moonshine I guess.

Majnu ka tila has undergone a sea change these days, and the shanty town has transformed into an upmarket backpackers haven, serving global cuisine, much like Thamiel of Kathmandu or similar hippy towns in Leh, Goa,

Hampi or Gokarna. There are Korean, Lebanese, Italian, and even Tibetan restaurants here, and you can order Sezu, Craft beer or Australian wine but not Chang any more. For that we have to travel to the hills.

However, in the higher altitudes, among the Sherpas, the Bhutias, the Lepchas and the Bhots, in places like upper Nepal, North Sikkim, Bhutan, where the terrain and climate does not support rice cultivation, another really exotic spirit cheers and warms the population. This too is called Chang, but there the similarity ends. My story is about this Chang, a true spirit for the roof of the world.

My first encounter with this brew was in Yuktham, in North Sikkim. Those days North Sikkim did not have hotels or resorts, and we were staying in a homestay, long before airbnb made it a household word. Basically villagers let tourists stay in their huts and eat in their kitchen. It was a wonderful experience, sharing the lives of these remote hill tribes, eating their food along with them in their kitchen, crowded around a roaring fire while it snowed outside.

There was a single very hazardous road linking North Sikkim to the rest of the country, and it was advised that we have a tribal guide or driver, as the Nepalese from Sikkim were very unwelcome by the original population, now relegated to North district, and they resented their loss of Kingdom and merger with India. We accordingly hired a Lepcha driver, and my attempts to learn his language quickly won the affections of this simple hills man.

That evening, after a hair raising and unbelievably picturesque drive, he dropped us off at our host's cottage, and invited me to join him in the village pub to meet his friends. I happily agreed.

We walked straight into what looked like a scene from an Indiana Jones film. A low dark stone hut lit by smokey oil lamps, where the guests were seated on the floor on thick Yak skins, with a wooden slab in the center acting as a communal table. A plump lady in exotic traditional robes was serving, and a fire in a stone hearth on which a battered samovar was steaming was making the place cosy.

When I followed the driver's lead and ordered a Chang, he was extremely happy. Apparently tourists ordered the army rum or whiskey there on the rare occasions that they visited, and not the local beverage.

A large hollow bamboo, filled with some brown grains, which I learnt was fermented Maize, was put before us. The samovar was brought over, and our beaming hostess poured boiling water into the heap. A thin hollow bamboo was provided, which was to be used as a straw, to sip the resultant liquor, after allowing it to stew for a few minutes.

This was heavenly. This had Irish coffee beat hands down. The hot aromatic liquid goes down your throat, warming you up, and leaving a pleasant afterglow. As the brew gets over, more hot water is added, and a single bamboo jug lasts you a long time, after which the millet is replaced.

The atmosphere is heady. Sitting on Yak skins in a dimly lit hut on the high Himalayas, snow outside, flickering firelight, drinking Chang from Bamboo jugs through bamboo straws, with people in exotic costumes talking in strange languages.

As directed by my guide cum driver, I was a big hit among the locals by the simple expedient of saying "Jhu

Ley" with folded hands and grinning at everyone. Strange food from others plates were offered and accepted, to the extent of sharing bites of a whole grilled fish.

In the meanwhile hours had passed in companionable drinking while my family waited impatiently in our cottage. Ultimately our kind hosts brought them into our den, to a warm welcome from the local populace. LOH enjoyed the ambience but not the food and drink on offer. Finally we returned after many warm farewells and a last sip for the road, escorted back by half the revelers.

But the last word came from my disgruntled daughter who was eight, and very upset about being hauled out in the cold.

She asked her mother" I have known Papa for just eight years and I already can't stand him,

How did you tolerate him for so long?"

She still doesn't have an answer.

Chapter 50

THE HAUNTING

Once we spent an idyllic vacation staying in a lonely ramshackle hilltop cottage in the middle of forests in a remote corner of Uttarakhand.

Every night we had a bonfire, and people from the nearby village, which had only 25 families, would drop in for a chat, while we had the local wine, and stories of the forest and the supernatural were related. Under the stars, no light other than the fire, complete silence except for the crackling fire, it was magical.

The stories were all in first person, as everyone appeared to have had personal interactions with the spirit world, and spoke about it in a matter of fact manner. In that atmosphere it was all very real and believable.

As per folklore, all hilltops are the abode of fairies, and though they don't harm people, they play pranks. Our host shared stories of pranks being played on him when he first moved here. The fairies had to be propitiated before he could use it as a homestay.

Another advice was to never give lifts to strangers on lonely roads as they are inevitably ghosts. Of course on practical considerations too it's dangerous, people being far more dangerous than ghosts.

In the bright morning light such stories seemed like fairy tales, as they quite literally were, and we luxuriated having breakfast in the bright sun on the meadow with crisp clear air and a panoramic view of snow peaks in a giant semicircle.

Like all good things our vacation came to an end and we had to return to the hot polluted plains of North India.

We were advised to take a rarely used shortcut to save an hour and enjoy a very scenic drive. Armed with detailed directions and the Google maps we left after breakfast.

We did come across a well dressed gentleman asking for lift in the middle of nowhere, and ignored him.

After about an hour, during which we saw no other people or vehicles, when the map showed that our point of meeting the regular route was 7 kms away, it suddenly showed that we were 24 kms away and going in the wrong direction. We assumed that we must have missed a turn somewhere, and turned around with difficulty. After returning a few kms, the map guided us to take a narrow road, which we did and again got 7 kms remaining. We happily proceeded, but after a km or so, it ended on a cliff face.

Stunned, we turned back with great difficulty and returned to the earlier road and started going back the way we came.

The map again insisted that we are going the wrong way and guiding us back to the narrow path. Ignoring it we started going back the way we came, nervous now about reaching the plains in time to catch our train.

We suddenly spotted a villager walking along the road and stopped to ask him directions. He looked surprised and asked us why we were going in the opposite direction. We asked him if he would show us the way, but we couldn't follow his directions. So we asked him if we could drop him there. He said that he isn't going there but would show us the way, and got into the car with his scythe and rope.

We turned around again and went back in the original direction.

By now we had lost an hour going around in circles. Guided by this good Samaritan, we ignored the Google map and the little side road and continued downhill. Our guide was mystified by the voice of the Google lady giving directions, and said how would this angrez know the way?

We told him that she didn't and is telling us to go the other way.

Anyway, after a while he told us to stop and got off. We were protesting that he was supposed to guide us, but he pointed out that he had promised to show us our destination, not take us there.

He accordingly pointed out a few houses deep in the valley and said that that's your destination, just follow roads that take you towards it, keeping to roads going downhill.

He then took a footpath and started walking down.

We followed his advice and within fifteen minutes reached the main road, and suddenly the Google map stopped saying 28kms to destination and said that your destination is here.

From then on we followed well travelled roads and reached the plains in time.

We assumed that it was some glitch in the Google maps, but sometimes I wonder, was it a prank of the fairies?

Chapter 51

CLOSE ENCOUNTERS OF THE FINAL KIND

My daughter had written a story on death, at an age when one is not supposed to have such thoughts, and it disturbed me. It was brought about by a close brush with death that we both had, but our memories differed.

This is how I remember the incident.

We had been vacationing in Goa, and enjoying the usual water sports, beach hopping, sampling the exquisite local seafood cuisine and wine. All this, while chilling us out, was ravaging the purse considerably.

That day, there seemed to be a storm shaping up, and the sea was quite rough. There were very few boats out, and even they were hurrying back. Warning was being issued on the loudspeakers for bathers not to venture out to sea. My wife was in a shack on the beach, reading, while I was in the surf with my kids.

That was when a boatman approached us, offering to take us parasailing for a ridiculously low rate, as he couldn't get customers. We had been parasailing earlier at many times the cost and agreed instantly.

Years ago, while hang gliding in Himachal, a similar offer from a guide on a stormy day had been turned down by my wife, and a couple who were in the same hotel as us had succumbed to the temptation, leading to the young man plunging to his death. This time she wasn't around to prevent such idiotic rashness, and I did not remember the incident till much later, and we heedlessly boarded the speedboat.

The waves were very high, and the boat was being tossed around more than any amusement park thrill ride, or grade four white water rafting. I was joking with my kids that this was extra thrills for free, as we screamed in excitement when getting buffeted and drenched by the breakers.

When the waves started going over our heads, I held on to my little girl, who was small and frail, and I thought she may get swept away. My elder daughter, tall, strapping and athletic, and an excellent swimmer, I wasn't worried about.

All of a sudden, a colossal wave flipped over our speedboat like a toy, and boatman screamed "jump!", and dived overboard. I held on to my little one and followed them.

We were lost in a dark green world being tossed around by enormous forces, and fighting for breath. But through it all, I kept my grip on my baby with all my strength. After what seemed like an eternity, we broke surface, among swirling waves, with no one else in sight. In desperation, I tried to dive underwater to search for my elder daughter, without letting go of the child. But our lifejackets kept pushing us up. Then an extra strong wave tossed us around and broke my grip. This time, I was back in the dark currents, helpless, and alone.

Life did not flash before my eyes, nor did any foreboding of death enter my mind, but my only thought was: how would I tell my wife that I have lost her babies?

Through the gloom I could see the boat, upside down, sinking to the bottom and trailing the parachute ropes. Then I thought I saw a hand reaching out for help. But the currents wouldn't let me reach her.

When I came up for air, I could see no one, and had no idea which way the shore would be. Suddenly, a head popped out, and it was my elder daughter, barely conscious, a few feet away. I held on to her for dear life, looking around for signs of my baby. When we crested a high swell, I could see the distant shore, and a number of lifeguard's boats coming towards us. I also saw the lead boat pick up a tiny figure in a red lifejacket from the sea. The baby was safe. Being light, the waves had pushed her a hundred yards towards the shore, as the lifejacket kept her on the surface. She was the first to be rescued. Now all we had to do was stay afloat and hold on to each other, and in five minutes we were being pulled aboard.

In the medical tent on shore we reunited with the younger kid, who wanted to know why I was trying to drown her till she got away and was saved by the boat uncle. The older one, once revived, wanted to kill our boatman, who was pleading with us not to lodge a complaint, as he would lose his licence and livelihood.

I learnt that the boat had flipped on the side that my elder daughter was sitting in, and she was trapped below it. However, she kept her nerve and managed to fight her way out untangling herself from the ropes, and fighting the strong back current at the depths to push herself up. She had nearly blacked out from holding her breath for so long. She was bruised and had rope burns, but her feisty spirit was back.

I later learnt that she felt forsaken that I had exercised a Sophie's choice, and tried to save my younger, and according to her, my favourite child.

In the meanwhile, my wife, oblivious to all this, was lost in some fictional drama, and our reappearance with a crowd of onlookers in tow, looking, well, like survivors of a shipwreck, shocked her out of the make believe word. And our story reinforced her healthy distrust of the liquid element, which had kept her onshore in the first place.

In order that fear doesn't paralyse us, we went parasailing again next day, at fine weather, and with a safer boatman.

My daughter's reaction and recollection of the same event is provided in the link below.

https://soumyamukherjee8.wordpress.com/2013/11/15/this-is-an-essay-by-my-daughterabout-an-incident-involving-us-both-my-memory-was-different-sharing-her-version-in-my-blog/

Much later, when watching the Amir Khan Starrer thriller Talash, the scene where he is diving underwater to find his lost child, resurrected my old nightmares.

But contrary to all clichés, our close brush with the reaper did not change us in any way, and we continued to live out our mundane lives like we are immortal.

Chapter 52

THE CUSTODIAN

This story, in a rough form, was narrated to me by a fellow traveller, around a campfire, in a forest. It totally intrigued me. I cannot verify its authenticity, but it rang true. The cliché that truth is stranger is quite true. I have related it here, with some literary licence. It is in first parson for better impact.

It was the worst trip of my life. My guardian angel was working overtime battling some ancient curse which was determined to end my young life or so it seemed.

I was a marketing executive touring Himachal, when electrifying news came from Delhi, that my imminent parenthood is getting pre-poned by a fortnight and if I did not rush back, I would miss the most significant event of my life. So, I decided that economizing be dammed and bought an air ticket to Delhi.

The day dawned with terrible weather & the flight from Delhi, which was to take me back to the most anticipated event of my life was getting delayed. My frustrating visit was shared by two anxious co- passengers, a Punjabi fellow salesman and a Gujarati realtor.

The Punjabi gentleman in his eagerness to meet targets, had missed his previous marriage anniversary – his first & missing his second, he feared might make him single again. He was cursing the weather for ruining his marriage.

Mehtabhai having concluded some business in HP was keen to return to a property deal and delay would cause losses which was like losing a limb to him. To our combined horror, it was announced that the flight from Delhi could not land and has flown back. SO we were left to try our luck the next day.

We three then decided to en- cash our tickets and hire a taxi at whatever rates available, to be shared by us three desperate people. That way, we could hope to reach Delhi the next morning.

As we started negotiations, a young lady approached us and requested that we let her be the fourth passenger. Gallantry and economy ensured that we agree to the proposition. We convinced a taxi to brave the weather for a small fortune and were relieved that we would be reaching Delhi soon. But weather and fate had other plans. A few miles from Bhunter, we were jolted by a crashing sound and saw the horrifying site of the hillside slowly collapse on the road, some boulders narrowly missing our vehicle.

The unnerved driver refused to proceed, offering us a ride back to town and when we refused, returned our money and left us stranded by the roadside. The lady too against our advice, threw her lot with us. She confided that she had with great difficulty convinced her parents to bless her engagement with a man from another community and the date set was tomorrow. Missing it she was convinced would leave her no option but to choose between family & beau, a choice she dreaded. So we waited for the road to be cleared, while trying to hitch lifts from the stranded trucks on the road. We finally convinced a very merry gentleman driving a fruit laden truck who had been making good use of the forced break journey by fortifying himself with liquid sustenance.

On our anxious inquiries about his ability to drive, he assured us he did not intend to but hand over the wheel to his apprentice, while he enjoyed well deserved siesta on the cabin roof. So the four of us squeezed into the cabin, the proximity being uncomfortable for the lady and guiltily pleasurable mixed with discomfort for us three. We were reconciled to finally reaching our destination late and exhausted but in time to avoid our personal disasters but the amount was not a spent force yet. A few hours later just as it was getting dark, we were dozing off and so was our designated driver. Speeding around a bend, he noticed when it was too late, another truck hurtling around the same bend from opposite direction. There was no time to brake, so he swerved left. Sitting by the window, I could see the truck veer inexorably towards the gorge to our left and felt the wheels slip off the road. The moment is indelibly frozen in my memory. It seemed to be happening in slow motion. The truck was slowly toppling left into the gorge. My mind was absolutely clear. We were going to die. My companions, jolted out of a doze had not quite realized what was happening. The ad hoc driver was trying to jump off the truck on to the road. But my life was not flashing before my eyes as it was supposed to. My only thoughts were 1. I will not see my child. 2. How will my wife bring up the child all alone?

But my guardian angel had not called it a day either. Instead of a free fall into the void, the truck stopped with a huge thump. There was a six feet ledge of terraced cultivation, six inches below road level. The truck was stuck, veering crazily in a small field of maize. Shocked out of the daze, we all scrambled out of the Drivers side, shaken and stirred but in one piece and jumped on the road. Other trucks had stopped and people were gathering. We noticed that ten feet ahead, the ledge ended and had we gone off the road a second later, we would be deep down in the gorge and up again towards our respective heavens or hells.

On head count we realized that truck owner was missing & feared the worst. But there is a special God for the inebriated and we found him sprawled in the field of maize looking dead. On closer inspection, he proved to be still peacefully sleeping. People really helped, perhaps the presence of the lady inspired chivalry. Some construction crew came with their equipment & helped haul the truck back on road. The spilled goods were reloaded. The engine was working fine and now sober driver took to the wheels. The spilled sacks were reloaded with lots of volunteer labour including us. We got back on the truck and journey resumed late in the night.

Early next morning, as dawn was breaking, we were at ISBT waiting for our auto, tired, dirty but ecstatic to be almost home. We now had to part ways and go to our respective lives. Having been through hell together was a bond and contacts were being exchanged. The lady wanted to visit the washroom to freshen up and. asked us to closely guard her belongings, as it had all her valuables for the coming ceremony. I jokingly told her not to trust strangers with such precious burdens, as we may just disappear. She said, " Look as I have trusted my most valuable possession, myself, in the custody of three strange men through the day & night of hell, in the most desolate of areas, in comparison these material possessions are nothing. I can trust you with them, and you are welcome to them if you so desire." We were left without an answer.

POST SCRIPT

A few days later, she came to visit my daughter in the nursing home (I had been present at this most exhilarating & frightening moment when I became a dad) and we three with our family were guests at her wedding a month and a half later. Mr. Singh & Mr Mehta too are still occasionally in touch.

Tears have gone by, but my most memorable journey refuses to fade from my memory.

Chapter 53

MEMORABLE MEALS I HAVE HAD

I am a foodie. My girth gives credence to the fact. But when I try to remember specific feasts, it is not the quality of the meals, and definitely not the quantity, but the associated memories, the ambience, the locale, the company and the circumstances in which they were enjoyed that make them memorable. Often it was poor fare by any gourmet standards or any standards at all, but the enjoyment derived beats Michelin rated chefs hollow. Not that I usually dine in that style, but had the good fortune of sampling a few. Enough of this preamble; Listed are some meals I vividly remember, despite being in an elevated spiritual plane when partaking in them.

In no particular order——

Dal bati and chach—1983 Ranthambore

Venue- a remote hamlet near Ranthambore in Rajasthan.

Ambience-Squatting on the mud floor, being served by giggling veiled women.

Company- three more backpackers, from Shillong, Mumbai and Australia respectively.

Hosts-A bevy of Rajasthani belles, wives and daughters of illegal wood gatherers and herdsmen, giggling behind their veils, and conversing through sign language and an incomprehensible dialect.

Menu- Lumps of dough made of Bajra, roasted directly on wood fire, crumbled with homemade ghee, and some sort of lentil. This is dal bati, a rural Rajasthani staple, one helping of which is enough to bloat a city dweller. This is washed down with buttermilk or chach in huge brass tumblers. Even the chillum enhanced appetite wasn't sufficient to consume more.

Charges- Free.

This was during a backpacking trip in Rajasthan, when we were denied legal entry in the Tiger Reserve and given shelter by complete strangers in a nearby hamlet. The ladies fed us, found our demeanor and appetites hilarious, when we showed helplessness in having more than one helping. Purdah was maintained by them staying just indoors and roaring with laughter from behind ghunghats, or veils. We were referred to as" Bawre"-the crazy ones. We slept in their courtyard, and later entered the forest illegally with their men folk, carrying a packed lunch of chana and gur, or, as the Aussi called it, Nuts and sugar. Suggestions of reimbursement of costs waere considered extreme bad manners as we were guests.

Goat intestine, red rice and Ghanti –1986 Kalpa

Venue-a high altitude village in the Kinnaur region in Himachal Pradesh.

Ambience-Dancing in the moonlight in a grassy knoll, snow peaks all around, beautiful Kinnauri belles forming long swaying human chains.

Company- my 12 fellow trekkers (including my wife) and most of the Kinnauri villagers gathered for the Poornima Mela or full moon fair.

Hosts-the entire village represented by their Headman.

Menu-Ghanti, which is a sort of apple cider, goat intestine cooked I don't know how.

This was the 12th day of the Kinnaur Kailash trek, courtesy Indian Mountaineering Federation, in the inner line area of Kinnaur. As in those days the area was inaccessible and prohibited to tourists, locals had not met outsiders and at every camp we were greeted by the nearest village and joined in on their impromptu singing and dancing to folk songs around campfires drinking prodigious amounts of Ghanti, which is the local brew made from apples and apricots. But the grand finale was the new moon fair, where we were special invitees and honored guests. A goat was sacrificed, and after many hours of inebriated dancing and singing incomprehensible songs, we had the starter made of goat's intestines and some kind of red rice or grain washed down with even more ghanti, till I passed out. I was later carried back to camp in procession by the villagers singing improper Bengali songs I had taught them.

Unidentified meat, rice and Millet Chang —2001 Yumthang

Venue- The village drinking hole in a small hamlet in North Sikkim.

Ambience- Low smoky stone room with a blazing fire on which cauldrons are bubbling, squatting on Yak skins on low stools with a bench in front, old lady in exotic garb smiling and serving, crowd of Lepcha villagers quizzing us in unknown tongue, and we are responding with the two Lepcha words we know.

Menu- Chang, served as a pile of fermented millet heaped in a large cut bamboo, into which boiling water is poured from a battered ancient brass samovar, and the resultant concoction is sipped through thin bamboo pipes. Accompanied by bits of meat of which you can't guess the origin.

Company—my wife, daughter, our driver cum guide and local Lepcha villagers.

In North Sikkim during a home stay in this high altitude village, this was the most exotic pub I have seen, which includes Indiana Jones films.

Fish Crab and Unknown Bird, Roasted on open Fire and river chilled Mahua – Jona, Jharkhand, 2002.

Venue-open air among rocks and roaring water, at the Jona falls near Ranchi.

Ambience- – Bathing in the falls, deserted thanks to fear of Maoists. The lone tribal man fishing and trapping in the river turned out not to be a terrorist but a gracious villager who offered to share his meal.

Menu- freshly caught fish and crab, gutted, stuck on sticks and roasted on an open fire. Ditto small bird trapped or shot with sling. Served on leaves. Washed down with Mahua, the delicious elixir made from the red flowering tree, which intoxicates elephants, bears, deer, monkey and birds, from old beer bottles, cooled in the rushing stream.

Company- My colleague from Ranchi who knew of this place, and the suspected red menace.

Having a day to kill after a business trip to Ranchi got over early; we visited the now deserted Jona falls and had this memorable experience which made me miss the flight back. Our tribal host was happy with whatever we offered him. He didn't ask, nor demur, nor bargain, merely gravely accepted whatever was offered.

Nun Cha, and Mathi in Kashmir—2013

Venue- a Kashmiri wooden house in a village, somewhere enroute Gulmarg.

Ambience- Squatting on a carpet in the central room of the traditional house, surrounded by a bevy of stunning women, please note no burkha or veil, all relatives of our driver, being quizzed as the first outsiders or Indians as they called us, to ever visit their home.

Menu- Salt tea or Nun cha, a Kashmiri staple not available in shops, which involves night long soaking and hours of boiling, and is more like soup, and Mathi, or home baked salted pastries.

It happened by chance, when stopping for Kava after a Wazwan at well known eateries enroute Gulmarg. Our driver, whom my wife suspected of being a terrorist, confided on quizzing that this isn't what they have at home. When I wanted to sample home fare, he invited us home. Leaving the main road, and finally the car, we walked down narrow lanes to the wooden house, our host answering every villager's questions on the way. His sister hosted the tea party, and everyone posed for photographs. Other than security forces on search operations, we were the first outsiders in their village in three decades.

Scrambled eggs, Sausages, and bread and an array of liquid, herbal and chemical elixirs for spiritual upliftment and expansion of consciousness.—Delhi 1985

Venue- my barsati bachelor pad in Delhi.

Ambience- impromptu pot luck party which was also my wedding feast.

Company- my new bride and a whole bunch of disreputable friends.

Menu- being pot luck, everyone brought something to ensure high spirits, whether liquid, solid or whatever, but no one remembered food. A sober neighbour went out and got a lot of eggs, sausages, bread and butter and that was the meal that cheered everyone but my wife.

Being a sudden decision and being broke, my post elopement party went like this. We left a room and terrace full of comatose people and went to face my unsuspecting parents and furious in-laws.

Chapter 54
A HUMAN GESTURE

During the recent catastrophe that hit our country, the entitled classes in urban India exposed their true nature. The obscenely rich tycoons, the privileged babus, the glitterati, the chattering classes, the ivory tower intellectuals, the drawing room socialists, and the political parties all displayed their utter callousness, complete selfishness and criminal disregard for those that served them. The underclass, the unseen wheels that keep our world running smoothly, were abandoned to their fate.

The media highlighted stories of misery of the abandoned migrant workers trudging home across India, perishing by the wayside, rioting for their rights and other such glimpses of human ignominy.

But what was largely ignored by the mainstream media with their political agenda, was the unprecedented help from ordinary citizens on the way, the good Samaritans spread out across rural Bharat. When reported on the discredited social media, urban sceptics from the privileged classes disbelievingly cried fake news.

I did not find this natural magnanimity unusual at all, having come across such good Samaritans everywhere in

India, among the ordinary people, usually far from the teeming metropolises.

Waiting for a bus in Kalpa at Kinnaur on the way back from a trek and finding no seats, we found the locals get off and offer us the seats, saying that they would go the next day.

Being offered food by complete strangers, and often a bed to spend the night, and refusing payment later, was something we experienced in Himachal, Uttarakhand, Rajasthan, Sikkim, Ladakh, Assam, Tamil Nadu, Jharkhand, Kashmir and Madhya Pradesh.

In a remote Kinnaur village we were invited to a festival, and a villager killed his goat to give a meal to twelve alien trekkers whose language they did not know.

Near Chail, a shopkeeper gave shelter to a drenched family, offered dry clothes, tea, and went out in the downpour to call a vehicle from our hotel and refused payment saying that we were in distress and it was his duty to help.

In Kodaikanal, stranded in a downpour, a dhaba owner offered us a place to sleep and a drunk stranger finally drove us to our hotel for free.

In Sikkim and in Assam, we were not charged for our meal at a roadside dhaba as we ordered local cuisine, and they shared their family's meal, and we did not order the tourist fare.

In Kashmir, tense with insurgency, our driver took us to his village for an authentic home meal as his guests.

In a deserted stream in Jharkhand, a man we were fearing as a Maoist, shared his catch of fresh fish cooked over fire with us and refused payment.

In a Rajasthan village, four strangers including an Australian were offered dinner, a place to sleep, and food packed for the journey the next day and they wouldn't accept any compensation from us saying that we were guests.

There have been numerous times when we received help from strangers on the highway when our vehicle broke down, tires got punctured or we were stranded by landslides or weather, I have lost count.

In Ladakh a passing mechanic took two hours to fix our bike and didn't accept a fee.

Near Draz, stranded by an avalanche, we got dinner and a place to stay in the local army camp as unannounced guests of the army.

Once late night, some drunken workmen fixed a leaking fuel pipe on my car, and refused payment because there was a child in the car, while I was suspecting them of trying to rob us.

The biggest lesson came from a truck driver. On a dark rainy night on a highway my silencer hit a rock, came off and was dragging behind emitting sparks. A truck stopped and two shrouded men came out. I was petrified as my wife and child were with me. These kind men took out the silencer, put it in the back seat after an hour long struggle in the dark, and turned down the money I offered saying this is the rule of the highway, and if they were stranded I would have also helped. I was too ashamed to say that I wouldn't even have stopped. Perhaps he knew this as well, but was too polite to say so.

Which is why when I hear these stories of the unknown unsung Samaritans sharing their little with these strangers, it doesn't surprise me in the least.

Nor does it surprise me that the Gurdwaras are doing an exemplary job in feeding these unfortunate migrant marchers. Various organisations are doing a fabulous job too, away from the limelight, including the much maligned RSS.

I know that there is hope, Bharat is resilient, and we will survive, bruised but not broken.

Chapter 55

MEMORIES OF A COLD DESERT

It is a dry, barren, grey landscape. I am wandering around. It is cold. Breathing is strained. Suddenly, I see this small dust cloud growing bigger. I try to run towards it, but I am exhausted after a few steps. The vehicle passes by leaving me behind. I shout out, but the noise from the vehicle in the quiet valley drowns my voice. I realize that it was you in the vehicle. I wake up.

I am sitting all alone, on the banks of this beautiful river. Only the soaring mountain, glowing in the setting sun, reflecting on the mirror-like surface of the water, is keeping me company. Suddenly, there is a whisper, 'It is getting cold, let us go inside'. I look up, and I see you. You have a warm yet fuzzy smile, curving on your lips. I wake up, again.

The place seemed to be calling me. And it seemed that you were there too.

I have wanted a 'trip' with you for more than twenty years now. I have felt this 'only if' feeling while traveling the world. I have, and I still feel this sense of everyday restlessness. The thought of this up till now unfulfilled fantasy pervades every moment of my life. The idea comes to me as often and as effortlessly as breathing. For many years, the place I wanted to get lost in with you was Ladakh. Now it is Spiti.

And it is only now that I truly understand why - why these landscapes beckon.

Spiti, in many ways, is like our relationship. Mostly empty, barren and cold yet everlasting and strangely beautiful. Often times, I find it difficult to breathe. Nevertheless, with a brilliant night sky and the stars almost at touching distance. Boulders are strewn everywhere, but with brilliant hues on bare rocks. Scarcely peopled, mostly rocky, and ground by glaciers for millions of years. The soil is all-encompassing - sandy, gravelly and yet rich. In the rare places where a bit of water has collected from the melting glaciers, there is a burst of green.

Does not all this seem eerily familiar?

There is a petrol pump-cum-provisions store in Spiti that says, 'last place to fill up fuel, provisions, and water. No human habitat or facility for the next 450 kilometers'. I do not have to tell you — but only the adventurous and the lonely venture there. There are no roads in that part of the valley. The road abruptly ends in a wasteland. I know that feeling. I want to wish it away.

Let us embark on this 'pilgrimage of the souls'. You and me. Let us start our journey in the middle of the clutter of the 'millennium city'. And keep moving until we get lost in Spiti's austere landscape. Let us leave behind the rattle of this shallow realm and strive to listen to the frail yet meaningful voices of our spirits. I want to see beyond the 'you' that the world knows. I want to experience the 'you' as you were crafted by nature. I want you to know the 'you' whom you have not conversed with in a long time. Until such time as you were ruined by the ways of this contrived world.

Let us go through our own share of 'vipassana'. Knowing well that we are living and breathing under the same sky, just a few steps away from each other, we should meet only once a day. Just like the rare glimpses of water and greens in Spiti's cold desert landscape. Knowing well that we have utter nothingness around us to fill with until now unspoken words, let us not speak. For mere words are often deeply inadequate for true expression. Knowing well, that our outer forms are longing for carnal intimacy, let us not touch. For when you lay your bloodshot eyes on me, you stir me in more ways than the world will ever know.

Spiti beckons – to let overwhelming emotions take over us, as we sit next to each other, staring into the blank bleak landscape. Spiti beckons – to teach us a lesson about the triviality of our outwardly form, and the true calling of our chi. Spiti beckons – to remind us, that you truly, only, live once…